S

THE SECRET TO CUSTOMER LOYALTY

SERVICE CERTAINTY

C

JASON FORREST
FPG

PAUL CARDIS
Avid Ratings

Printed by MJS Press
Printed in U.S.A

International Standard Book Number: ISBN 978-0-692-78924-7

TABLE OF CONTENTS

A NOTE FROM JASON & PAUL

And the answer to the question: "Is reading this book worth my time?"

We used the editorial "we" in this book, but for personal stories and examples, we used "I" to indicate who was involved.

When you change the way you look at customer service, customer service changes.

If you're trying to decide whether to invest valuable time in reading further, let us make it simple:

> 1) If you want to use exaggerated or coerced ratings to create the illusion that your customers are delighted, this book isn't for you.

> 2) If you want to check "receive customer feedback" off of your to-do list, put this book down right now.

> 3) If you are looking for a band-aid to cover up poor culture or business practices, don't waste another minute.

If, on the other hand, you are ready to revolutionize your approach to customer service, you are in the right place. And if you want to create operational excellence verified through honest evaluations of your customer experiences, this book will change the very core of how you do business. If that's what you're looking for, by all means, read on.

Nobody raves about being mildly pleased or goes out of their way for a good meal. For a *great* meal though, people will drive across the country. This is the heart of service certainty: providing an experience so unique and unforgettable that customers feel personally connected to and invested in it. A homebuilder who successfully cultivates service certainty ends up with committed and deeply loyal buyers who naturally express that loyalty through high survey scores, positive customer reviews, and frequent referrals.

~

We'd like to give you a little insight into our unique backgrounds and experience, including how we got into the business, how our paths crossed, and why we are qualified to talk about this subject.

Though we represent different parts of the homebuilding industry, we each bring a unique understanding of today's challenges as well as experience to overcome them. Jason is a behavior change expert and Paul is a customer experience expert. Together, we create solutions and behavioral change programs that transform company cultures and improve individual and organizational performance (and therefore profitability) for homebuilders.

As Avid Ratings' founder, Paul helps organizations understand and improve the customer experience. For the past 24 years, he has worked with the industry's leading homebuilding companies to measure the customer experience and transform many that started with the lowest customer experience scores to become those with the highest.

Through homeowner surveys, Avid Ratings gathers the most comprehensive data in the industry. While the numbers do give us a window into the customer's experience, the ultimate goal isn't just to have satisfied buyers and survey results that look nice on a website. It's for homebuilders to have an internal brand that embodies service certainty and an expression of that brand through each company representative.

Without a whole-company approach (starting with leadership!), customers will never be truly happy, which is why Jason's contributions on behavior change are so important. Jason's industry wisdom starts with his years as a front-line sales professional. He evolved through both his successes and failures and now learns from participating in the same processes on an organizational level—observing winning and failing company strategies and gaining greater understanding of what works on a cultural level. Jason's experience indicates that results can always be traced back to beliefs. Without changing beliefs, behaviors never sustainably change. That's why so many of the following pages are devoted to rethinking, reconditioning, and redefining.

Our paths crossed when Paul was looking for the best training company to recommend to clients. He chose Forrest Performance Group (FPG) because of the overlapping philosophies and the complete behavior-change solution. Likewise, the customer experience is a natural complement to culture training because it provides a benchmark to evaluate progress. But with fraudulent reviews (by both builders and survey companies) running rampant, Jason needed assurance that Avid's approach was honest. Avid's commitment to full disclosure of customer feedback appealed to Jason. The partnership was a perfect fit.

This book represents the knowledge we have gained from years of steadfast effort to improve the industry (rather than just hanging some window dressing) and reflects the realities of improving the customer experience in our unique industry. Between us, we have faced countless boardroom meetings and individual customer challenges, plus 10,000+ hours of coaching conversations with real-life builder representatives—from CEOs to salespeople.

Our combined decades of experience provide understanding about what it takes to make customers truly happy. It has taught us that the most complex problems often have simple solutions. We address the psychology of customer loyalty because happiness is in the mind. We want you, the reader, to come away with a deeper understanding of how happiness works.

We were compelled to write this because so many other books make the solution to customer loyalty way too complex. Buying a home is one of an individual's or family's most critical life decisions, and the sale can take up to a year. This makes its customer experience challenges different than for restaurants or resorts, for example, and increases the difficulty in keeping customers happy. Homebuilding is unique and therefore deserves unique attention. This is the first book to address those specific needs.

We wrote this book together because our backgrounds in strategy coupled with research provide a winning combination. The how-tos are supported by statistical evidence, which allows us to understand and prove the reasons (what we call the whys) behind those how-tos. Most solutions only address the how-tos.

Though we have somewhat different areas of expertise, we have a shared vision of how to create customer loyalty. We also have a common goal: making customers happy through operational excellence. We do this in an organic way rather than engaging in review fraud—a practice which is coming under review from the Federal Trade Commission (FTC).[1] Such fraud (called review scrubbing, or review washing) is still all too common among many companies, including builders. It happens when a company hires a third-party researcher to collect customer feedback but omits the negative reviews from the public's view, thereby falsely bolstering its overall score.

This book answers three guiding questions:

1) What are the simple strategies and solutions that create delighted customers and brand loyalty?

2) What is true customer service?

3) How can we create service certainty?

This book is about getting at the magic bullet that makes service certainty possible. It isn't about perfection 100% of the time, but about making customers happy in an imperfect world. It is possible. We promise.

~

Read on for an easy guide to creating truly delighted customers: 14 best practices that create service certainty and increase customer loyalty.

[1]Federal Trade Commission, "Guides Concerning the Use of Endorsements and Testimonials in Advertising," PDF file, last modified September 9, 2016, https://www.ftc.gov/sites/default/files/attachments/press-releases/ftc-publishes-final-guides-governing-endorsements-testimonials/091005revisedendorsementguides.pdf.

BEST PRACTICE 1
Get Your Mind Right About Customer Service

"Know your why."
-Adidas slogan

THE FIRST 2 STEPS TO MAKING YOUR CUSTOMER TRULY HAPPY

FOCUS ON COMPANY CULTURE 1

CHALLENGE YOUR BELIEFS 2

"In high school, football dominated my focus. No matter how much my parents and teachers stressed the importance of education, I just wanted to do what felt good to me at the moment. And that was blocking, tackling, and driving. That's all I needed to know. It wasn't that I couldn't do well in school; it's just that I didn't have the personal motivation to make it a priority. I didn't understand *why.*

But then the reality hit me that being a talented athlete with no job and no education wasn't going to be so cool when I was 25. Once I understood why it was important to apply myself in school, I didn't need my parents to be on my case or teachers reminding me to do my work. I just did it. I knew I needed to push myself academically to reach my professional goals. I didn't need anyone telling me what to do; I just needed to know for myself why to do it.

I believe in the mind's power so wholeheartedly that I personally hire coaches to help me where I'm weakest. I have (or have had) coaches for speaking, running my business, taking care of my health and more. I know there's a reason the coaches I choose are successful in their specialty areas, and if I can train myself to see as they see and think as they think, I can be successful too."

—Jason

As of this writing, Amazon.com lists more than 70,000 results for books on customer service.[2] Most address how to treat customers or what to say to set yourself up for positive survey responses and reviews. This book is unique because it addresses the why behind making customers truly happy. Digging into the why allows us to correct limiting beliefs, establish new beliefs, and make real, long-term changes. When a person's beliefs are in line, their behaviors follow. The right beliefs lead to the right behaviors, which increase service certainty and create addicted, loyal customers (rather than just nice-looking survey scores). Customers reach service certainty when they trust they've found a partner in their mission and when they are confident their builder and builder representatives will look out for their best interest.

Before diving into the best practices that will revolutionize what you believe about and how you approach customer service, commit to the following key steps:

What and how you think determines your success.

1) Focus on company culture.

Company culture is not just made up of the ideals that company leadership profess, but of each employee's beliefs. This is why builders, team leaders, and individuals cannot afford to ignore company culture. It's the one thing that makes everything else (brand loyalty and service certainty, for example) possible. You must actively build a culture that leads to customer loyalty. This isn't about creating a perception of having happy customers. It's about creating a culture that leads to the best possible customer experience, and therefore, truly delighted customers.

This is what we mean by service certainty. Service certainty is the foundation of the customer experience—only through creating psychological certainty can you cause delight and elation in the homebuying experience. Creating certainty is more important than the floor plans you develop, the land you buy, and the upgrades you offer. Company culture lays the foundation for true service certainty.

2) Challenge your beliefs.

We agree with Wayne Dyer's assertion: "If you change the way you look at things, the things you look at change."[3] The way we view things shapes every-thing—our behaviors and results included. Our beliefs permeate our approach to the world—work, home life, and everything in between. In order to truly effect change, we must change the way we see things. The most effective, longest-lasting way to change behavior is to change the way you see the world—the way you believe and think. It's a powerful thing: Programming drives beliefs, beliefs drive emotions, emotions drive behaviors, and behaviors drive results.

Customers reach service certainty when they believe their builder is a partner in their mission.

Instead of spinning our wheels addressing behaviors (our own or someone else's), we advocate for working on programming by teaching and adopting new beliefs. From there, behaviors follow. And new behaviors cause new results.

~

Seeing things differently can genuinely lead to a better life. What we believe, how we feel, what we think, and how we see ourselves all have more influence over our success than anything else. Even our abilities fade in importance. And best yet, when our beliefs are in line, they drive the behaviors that lead to service certainty in our customers. They feel assured and comfortable with every step of the process. So let's talk about culture, beliefs, customer needs, and the practical solutions that lead to addicted, raving fans—advocates for our products and communities!

[2] Accessed July 14, 2016, https://www.amazon.com/s/ref=nb_sb_ss_c_1_22?url=search-alias%3Daps&field-keywords=customer+service+books&sprefix=undefined%2Caps%2C251.

[3] "When You Change the Way you Look at Things," video file, April 19, 2008, https://www.youtube.com/watch?v=urQPraeeY0w.

BEST PRACTICE 2
Make Feedback Work for You

"The trouble with most of us is that we would rather be ruined by praise than saved by criticism."

-Norman Vincent Peale

THE 3 STEPS TO MAKING FEEDBACK WORK FOR YOU

GET YOUR MIND RIGHT ABOUT FEEDBACK **1**

GET YOUR MIND RIGHT ABOUT SURVEY TALK **2**

CAMPAIGN TO INFORM **3**

"A homebuilder came to Avid in dire straits. Though public relations damage had already been done, they were looking to improve the homebuyer experience and regain community trust.

The builder's nightmare started when a customer had a major mechanical issue in his new home. What began as a seemingly standard warranty concern became aggravated when he tried to repair the problem himself—causing further damage and voiding the warranty in the process.

While the builder was within its contractual rights to reject his demands (which it did), the buyer then had a much bigger problem than the mechanical one—a major beef with the builder. He set about seeking revenge.

To publicize his dissatisfaction, the homebuyer filled his pickup truck with 10,000 lemons and dumped them on his front lawn. He invited the local media, who responded in droves to the spectacle of a yard full of rotting produce and angry signs. Every station gave him airtime to describe his perception of the builder's failures. The debacle cost the company many times the value of the disgruntled buyer's house.

The builder used the situation as an opportunity to get feedback, change practices, and improve their customer experience."

—Paul

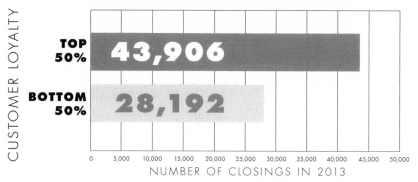

HOMEBUILDERS' CUSTOMER SATISFACTION SCORES IN RELATION TO NUMBER OF CLOSINGS

CUSTOMER LOYALTY

TOP 50%: 43,906

BOTTOM 50%: 28,192

0 — 5,000 — 10,000 — 15,000 — 20,000 — 25,000 — 30,000 — 35,000 — 40,000 — 45,000 — 50,000

NUMBER OF CLOSINGS IN 2013

Source: Avid Award

The builders in this study were divided equally into two groups based on the overall satisfaction score. Homebuilders scoring in the top 50% versus bottom 50% were then tallied to see how many homes they delivered during the past year. The results show that the top scorers in customer satisfaction build considerably more homes than those in the bottom half, indicating a possible positive relationship to making customers happy and building/selling more homes.

When customer relationships go sour, it costs more than any builder can afford. And we're not just talking about money. Even mildly unsatisfied buyers threaten future business, but the angriest buyers will actively work to tarnish a builder's most valuable assets—their reputation and brand.

It's stories like the one that opened this chapter that led to Avid's creation. Builders want to know how to create an experience customers will rave about. They want to develop a reputation they can build their own future success on, and they need delighted customers to make this happen. In order to have and keep delighted customers, they have to get and listen to authentic reviews. Everybody says they want honest customer feedback, but a company's future and its custo- mers' certainty depend on its commitment to get authentic feedback and then use it to drive change. Follow these steps to make feedback work for you:

1) Get your mind right about feedback.

While the FTC prosecutes companies for publishing ratings to reflect high scores when the actual reviews indicate otherwise,[4] many companies give in to the temptation anyway—especially when faced with unfavorable customer feedback. In a *New York Times* article, David Streitfeld gives the example of a charter bus company that received consistently low ratings. Instead of taking responsibility and fixing the issues, the chief executive "hired freelance writers, mandated that his employees write favorable reviews and even pitched in himself."[5]

He was viewing feedback all wrong. Instead of using the results to improve the customer experience, he sabotaged future success by compromising the company's culture and reputation. Unfortunately, builders also fall prey to fabricating results. Unscrupulous research providers wanting to make a quick buck encourage builders to falsify their overall performance—a compelling temptation for many.

SALES CONVERSION...

THE CONVERSION RATE FOR REFERRAL PROSPECTS IS TWICE AS HIGH AS FOR MARKETED PROSPECTS.

Source: Avid Ratings, based on a regional study of sales traffic conversion.

Surveys are so popular because, in theory, they provide valuable insights for companies looking to improve customer relations. But when results are corrupted, they leave companies worse off than they started—with a falsely positive view of their customers' experience rather than a true reflection of what they're doing well and what they could do better.

We've got to think about feedback differently. Instead of hiding from the truth (or manipulating it and losing our integrity), we need to see it as an opportunity to improve our customer experience and increase service certainty.

THE POWER OF REFERRALS

Percentage referred by:

● MARKETED PROSPECTS
● FRIEND/FAMILY MEMBER
● REALTOR REFERRAL

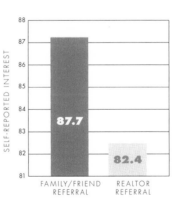

Source: Avid Ratings

Pie slices represent data collected nationwide across all Avid Sales Center Survey Program participants in 2010 and indicate their interest level on a 6 point Likert scale with 1 indicating no interest and 6 representing high interest. A separate study tracking conversion rates shows that those who were referred signed a purchase and sale agreement twice as often as those who were not referred, with 15.1% of referred prospects signing and 6.5% of marketed prospects signing.

2) Get your mind right about survey talk.

The president of a major homebuilder approached Avid, thinking survey was flawed. They had good scores in other areas, but their "recommend to friend" scores were stuck at 89 percent. His concern gave Avid pause. It's rare to have a builder score so well in lots of other areas without also scoring high on the "recommend to friend" question. After extensively interviewing employees and buyers, Avid couldn't identify the cause of this apparent glass ceiling. Finally, the president vented, "We do everything for these customers! We even go to every home right before your survey goes out to tell them how to fill the darn thing out."

AVID RATINGS STUDY

7.5% OF THE AVERAGE BUILDER'S
CUSTOMERS MADE A NEGATIVE REFERRAL.

AVID AWARD WINNERS HAD LESS THAN 1%.

Source: Avid Award

The mystery unraveled as he explained that the company trained superintendents to knock on every door and tell the buyers to fill out their survey with the highest scores and to check "definitely yes" by the "recommend to friend" question. They even dropped off a nice gift to each buyer for their willingness to provide high marks.

There it was. The builder did a good job with customers, so why did they feel the need to badger buyers door to door? By engaging in "survey talk" (any form of influencing responses), they caused mistrust among previously happy customers. If trust is lost, a company is in danger of becoming critically toxic. Avid advised the president to retrain employees and back off from the pressure tactics. The glass ceiling lifted immediately and their "recommend to friend" scores increased 8% in one year, earning them a "great" score on the survey and recognition in the top 10% nationwide.

A common myth in customer satisfaction is
that customers give higher ratings if pressured
to give a positive response.

Research shows that too much verbal pressure
from employees to give a positive response
results in lower customer satisfaction ratings.

It may seem harmless to say something like, "If there's any reason you can't give us 100%, give me a call before filling the survey out so we can make things better." But it feels manipulative to buyers and nobody benefits when people feel coerced into providing falsely positive results. Builders may be able to publish nice-looking numbers, but it's an expensive way to pat themselves on the back and carry on with the status quo.

The status is not quo.

The survey talk is counterproductive—a way to manufacture the appearance of a positive customer experience rather than doing what it takes during the preceding months to earn it. Although it may make builders feel good for a moment, the manipulated truth doesn't improve the company or brand.

SURVEY TALK: SURVEY AWARENESS VS. SURVEY PRESSURE

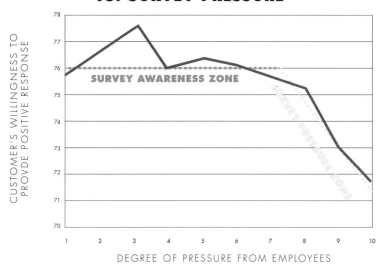

DEGREE OF PRESSURE FROM EMPLOYEES

Source: 2005 Avid Award Study presented by *Professional Builder*

3) Campaign to inform.

We're not advocating avoiding all survey discussion. Since 2002, Avid has been asking homebuyers, "To what degree did your builder pressure you to provide a positive response on this survey?" Scores from the two highest levels of influence show that overly aggressive survey talk results in lower ratings. Specifically, there was a significant drop in the "recommend" levels from the second highest to the highest levels of influence.[6] The bottom line: Builders who campaign too hard see diminishing returns.

Train employees to make sure customers are aware of surveys, but not to influence their responses. Controlled messages like letters, signs, and placards encouraging people to complete surveys increase response rates. A good awareness campaign simply lets people know the survey is coming and you're looking for honest, open feedback. That way, you can get the largest volume of valid responses without jeopardizing your integrity.

Survey Awareness is an important strategy for builders to maximize customer satisfaction results.

Survey Pressure can be detrimental to your relationship with customers and reduce your overall customer satisfaction ratings.

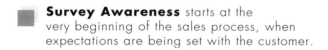

Authentic survey results make you better; Manipulated results are counterproductive.

Providing accurate measurement and results takes a lot of effort and time. But it's worth it because it's the only way to make surveys meaningful for customers and companies alike. Aggressive campaigns are both counterproductive and unnecessary when builders provide service certainty throughout the process.

Of course, accurate feedback only matters if we actually listen to it—the good, the bad, and the ugly. That's how companies improve and customers learn to trust us. Without trust, there can be no certainty. And when certainty is lost, all is lost. If you want addicted, raving fans, you have to earn trust organically.

Survey Awareness starts at the very beginning of the sales process, when expectations are being set with the customer.

[4] Courtney Rubin, "FTC Settles First Case in New Crackdown on Fake Reviews," *Inc.*, August 27, 2010, http://www.inc.com/news/articles/2010/08/ftc-settles-case-over-fraudulent-reviews.html.

[5] David Streitfeld, "Give Yourself 5 Stars? Online, It Might Cost You," *The New York Times*, September 23, 2013, http://mobile.nytimes.com/2013/09/23/technology/give-yourself-4-stars-online-it-might-cost-you.html?referrer=&_r=2.

[6] Paul Cardis, "If You Can't Give Me All 6's," *Professional Builder*, September 1, 2005, http://www.probuilder.com/if-you-cant-give-me-all-6s. Cardis specifies this was a statistically significant drop of 4.08 points (p<.001).

BEST PRACTICE 3
Create Certainty that Never Ends

"If you do what you did in the beginning of the relationship there won't be an end."
-Tony Robbins

THE 2 WAYS TO PROVIDE NEVER-ENDING SERVICE

BUILD LOYALTY TO YOU **1**

BUILD LOYALTY TO
THE LIFE THEY'LL LIVE
IN THEIR HOME **2**

"After a Fort Worth restaurant's grand opening, my wife and I were so excited for what we thought would become our new favorite place to eat. We were blown away by the food and the experience. After trying three more visits, we found we just didn't like it. We kept saying, 'I wish the food was as good as it was at the grand opening.'"

—Jason

When a new restaurant opens up, it gets all this special attention. Everyone is dying to walk through its doors and get a taste—not just of the food, but of the experience. Often, the first week is when the food tastes best, the presentation is sharpest, and customers get the best care. But if we wow customers on the first visit and disappoint them on the second, they won't become loyal fans. Giving our best only until the contract is signed is like a restaurant knocking it out of the park only at the grand opening: both will soon lose their luster along with their customers.

Treat customers like prospects and they'll never feel like "just" customers.

We must continue providing the same level of focus, attention, and care to customers under contract as we do to prospects. Prospects are glamorous, but customers are the ones paying the bills. And if we want customers to remain customers, we need to treat them like we did when they were prospects.

Buyers want their homes most at the moment they're signing the contract. It's also the moment their value peaks in builder representatives' eyes. Customers can sense when our interest wanes. On the other hand, if they feel just as wanted after they've contracted, we'll fend off buyer's remorse and the sense that, if they went to a competitor, they'd have a better experience.

Ongoing service pays off for builder representatives and creates service certainty in customers. Below are two ways to provide never-ending service:

1) Build loyalty to you.

One of the most basic and powerful approaches to business success is to copy successful people. And there's nobody with a better reputation for creating loyal customers than Joe Girard. Though he was honored as the "Greatest Car Salesman" by *The Guinness Book of World Records*, his success goes far beyond good salesmanship and demonstrates true customer service mastery. Girard sold 1,425 cars in 1973 and 13,001 over his 15-year career. According to Girard, though, he never sold a car, he sold himself. The most valuable products his customers walked away with were Joe Girard and his "service, service, service."[7]

Girard would say, "Today you bought two things. [The car and] Joe Girard. I'll tell you something else. If you happen to have gotten a lemon, as God is my judge, I am going to turn it into a peach. I am going to show you that I am different from any other salesman in the world. I will give you service like you never saw."[8]

Your goal is to create lifetime customers.

That kind of skin-in-the-game commitment increases certainty. Girard's famous line, "The sale begins after the sale,"[9] means he took permanent responsibility for the relationship and product. If customers had a problem, Girard was involved. He took care of the mechanics so they would take care of his customers. He never wiped his hands of the deal and every contact was as important as the first.

What if every employee fought over the opportunity to work customers through concerns rather than trying to hand them off to someone else? When customers feel their builder representatives value them more than their paychecks, they'll stick through the issues that are bound to come up and give positive responses on customer service surveys. And they won't be able to help but to share their experience with friends. In short, you will have created service certainty.

Girard's principles gained him endless return customers and referrals. Everyone who worked with him wanted their friends and family to have the same kind of great experience they did.

We've heard builders say their business is different from anyone else's and repeat customers don't matter for them. They say, "We're working with totally different people in different areas all the time. We can't get referrals." This is a sorry excuse for treating people poorly. To determine whether you've provided the kind of service that warrants repeat business, ask yourself, "If they could buy from us again, would they?" Whatever your answer is, it's part of your brand—individually and as a company. It affects you forever.

When we treat customers with the same reverence and respect as we did at the first encounter, we maintain a strong relationship well after the transaction is complete.

2) Build loyalty to the life they'll live in their home.

If we want loyal customers, we can't just get them excited about incentives, interest rates, and flooring options. Such circumstantial motivators have a place, but it's more important customers fall in love with the life they'll live in their new home than with the structure itself. If homebuyers picture raising their kids in the home and entertaining friends and family on the back porch, their commitment will go beyond a signature and will be etched into their hearts.

Buyers want their home most right before they sign the contract.

Unlike most industries, homebuyers don't walk away with a product in hand. After they sign, they may wait months to close and physically move in. Since their commitment is intangible, it is important to keep contracted customers positively engaged, both mentally and emotionally.

Buyers want their home most before they sign. After signing, their eyes naturally start to wander, and it's normal for customers to want the home just a little less. Combat this by talking about where they're going to put their furniture, who they'll have over, and the memories they'll make. Keeping them emotionally connected increases certainty about their decision. As long as they continue to mentally "own" the home, they'll be more likely to follow through with the final steps to owning the home physically.

If customers could buy from you again, would they?

~

Service is selling and selling is service. Whether you are in sales, design, warranty, or any other part of the business, look at each contract as "to be sold," not "to be built." If you don't, there's a good chance it'll end up as "to be cancelled." Creating certainty that never ends creates loyal fans and the kind of reviews that make people feel they simply have to buy from you. Remember Tony Robbins' mantra: "If you do what you did in the beginning of the relationship there won't be an end."

/ Amy Wilson, "Joe Girard, a Man for the Record Books, Sold 13,001 Chevrolets in 15 Years," *Automotive News*, October 31, 2011, http://www.autonews.com/article/20111031/CHEVY100/310319926/joe-girard-a-man-for-the-record-books-sold-13001-chevrolets-in-15.

II Ibid.

9 "Joe Girard," *Selling Power*, accessed June 15, 2015, http://www.sellingpower.com/content/article/?a=8598/ joe-girard/ &page=2.

BEST PRACTICE 4
Create Lollapalooza

"Excellence is to do a common
thing in an uncommon way."
-Booker T. Washington

THE 2 WAYS TO KEEP YOUR CUSTOMERS' LOYALTY AFTER CONTRACT

KEEP THE MAGIC ALIVE 1

BE PROACTIVE 2

"Adera Development (an award-winning builder in Vancouver, BC) invites employees, trade partners, and community members to an annual celebration called Adera Day. They provide free food, model home tours, and a fun, celebratory atmosphere. I joined them one year to speak about the customer experience—and wow! They didn't hold back. The owner and senior staff (dressed in workout clothes because they'd tried the new workout facility) spent the day in the middle of the fun, mingling and celebrating with people. This sort of event goes beyond a typical community opening or company event and creates the extra special feeling that you belong in a community. It was magic."

—Paul

We all want to be exceptional in our lives and work. We want to create lollapalooza—an extraordinary thing, event, or person. One of the best examples comes from "The Happiest Place on Earth": Disneyland.

It's more than a slogan. By creating a fairytale experience for millions of customers, Disneyland has earned a remarkable 70 percent first-time return rate.[10] Each employee shares a unifying purpose: to create magic. Every visit is designed to be a lollapalooza, with personalized experiences for young and old alike. Every detail matters.

When he was alive, Walt Disney himself greeted guests. Today, company leaders walk the parks, interact with guests, and pay close attention to customers' reactions to new rides. The execs are out among the people instead of tucking themselves away in a building far from the action.

Our challenge is to create our own lollapalooza brand. If we want to be like Disney, we have to act like Disney. Builder representatives can create lollapalooza experiences for each customer by providing a personal touch. Below are two ways to keep your customers' loyalty after contract and create lollapalooza beyond the closing:

Keep the magic alive each and every day.

1) Keep the magic alive.

In his book *Sprinkles*, author and business consultant Chip Bell calls the moments of magic we create "sprinkles."[11] They are moments of whimsy, of complete surprise. Frequent sprinkles increase loyalty and the customer's certainty that they made the right decision. Find opportunities to keep the magic alive after signing.

For example, celebrate the closing like you would if your best friend were moving into a new home. Instead of just passing the keys across the table, have salespeople, the superintendent, and the warranty representative meet owners at their new home. Make it an extraordinary event. Have a ribbon on the door and present customers with a welcome package that includes everything they need to know about the community. Provide information that makes it simple for them to set up utilities or manage other details to ease their transition. They will feel extraordinary and you will earn their loyalty, along with genuinely positive reviews.

2) Be proactive.

Sometimes it's the little things that build loyalty. Simply paying attention to customers and details turns the ordinary into the extraordinary. Look for opportunities to proactively and continually earn buyers' trust and confidence. Make them feel wanted during every step of the process. Have a finger on the pulse of each buyer—whether they're concerned or settled and what's keeping them up at night. When you do, you have a chance to ease their minds and achieve service certainty.

Be proactive, not reative.

We need to be like the company that sold Jason and Shelly their last home. During the entire process, their salesperson called every week with updates. She may have had something as minor to say as "The drywall went in!" or something bigger—that there was a hiccup in the process, for instance. But either way, seeing her name on the caller ID reassured them and brought certainty. She kept them in the loop without their needing to knock on her door.

Builder representatives who call before customers have a chance to notice a problem get brownie points. On the other hand, if customers have to bring up the concern or ask the question, builder representatives don't get credit—even if they solve the problem. Especially in roles like sales, design, and mortgage, it's great to make it a game to call customers before they have a chance to even identify a need.

The customers who call the most are the ones who feel they have to micromanage the process. Even if you solve their problems, they're not going to feel certainty through the process. They end up taking up the most time AND giving the worst scores.

~

To keep customers feeling certain in their decision, we must make the experience magical. Making each customer feel at home is true lollapalooza.

[10] Gregory Ciotta, "How Disney Creates Magical Experiences (and a 70% Return Rate)," *Help Scout*, June 11, 2004, http://www.helpscout.net/blog/disney-customer-experience/.

[11] Chip Bell, *Sprinkles*. (Austin: Greenleaf Book Group Press, 2015).

BEST PRACTICE 5
Build Customer Intimacy

*"Get closer than ever to your customers—
so close that you tell them what they need
before they realize it themselves."*
-Steve Jobs

THE 3 WAYS TO BUILD CUSTOMER INTIMACY

BE EMPATHETIC 1

BUILD OMAKASE 2

TREAT THE PERSON,
NOT THE DISEASE 3

"When we had our first baby, I wasn't fully prepared for how his ear-piercing, earth-shattering cries could bring our entire world to a halt. At first it seemed no movement or calming sound would do the trick. But often, as soon as he settled into my wife's arms or mine, he would instantly quiet down and be happy again."

—Jason

When babies cry relentlessly, they need a familiar, soothing touch to make the world right again. This touch stimulates the release of oxytocin—a hormone that promotes bonding.[12] The intimacy between a loving parent and child makes babies feel secure.

Similarly, each builder representative's care and attention makes buyers feel secure and creates customer intimacy—the certainty customers feel when they know their builder representatives understand their mission and are on their team to make it happen. Intimacy in any partnership requires trust and "mind sync"— being connected on a shared journey to accomplish a mutually beneficial goal. When customers have this intimacy with their builder, they feel secure because they have an advocate and partner in their mission.

When customers feel settled, they are more likely to respond well, even when there are delays and other unexpected events, because they trust their builder representative to take care of the issues.

There is a connection between what we do and the results we get.

Below are three ways to build customer intimacy:

1) Be empathetic.

In 1981, a man named Mehmet Ali Ağca shot Pope John Paul II four times. In the ambulance, as he suffered profound blood loss, the Pope pronounced his forgiveness. When he recovered, the Pope's top priority was to visit his attacker in jail. He wanted to see what was going on in Ağca's life to drive him to this act. Pope John Paul II ended up personally campaigning for Ağca's release, and his sincere compassion had a seemingly profound effect on the gunman, who requested to visit and lay flowers on the Pope's tomb years later.[13]

People aren't born mean, angry, or distrustful. But when an event occurs that programs us to distrust or react, we carry the experience into future circumstances. This is equally true for our customers. When they come in cursing and screaming, it's easy to get defensive and shut down instead of dealing with the situation con-structively. However, when we shift our perspective to one of empathy, we can approach customers with a true desire to understand, rather than defend. Then we are more likely to not just overcome the rough patch, but to forge a greater sense of intimacy. And in doing so, we may just earn loyal customers for life.

Empathy goes beyond saying words like, "I know buying a home is difficult." It's putting yourself in your customers' shoes and really appreciating that they're making big, emotional life decisions. When you understand, you're able to speak with them from the heart. And when you do, they have a lot harder time walking away from the contract because it would also mean walking away from a relationship they value.

Empathy increases certainty and makes customers feel important, understood, and safe, which increases loyalty to your brand.

2) Build omakase.

At Shinjuku Station, a Fort Worth sushi restaurant, customers who skip the menu and instead request *omakase* get the best experience. This Japanese word means "I leave it to you" and demonstrates a trusting relationship. By entrusting the owner, Casey Kha, and chefs to do what they do best, customers are rewarded with delicious, creative dishes and truly memorable dining.

Ask customers to allow you to help them make decisions. You know you're equipped to lead them to a solution they'll love—but they need to know that, too. Ask for their permission and they'll feel grateful to have found someone to lead them. It takes pressure off!

Have certainty in your product, processes and efficacy—just like a server who has full confidence in the menu is happy ordering for patrons. Your clients will readily hand off decisions to you because they recognize you know what's best. Confident builder representatives who consistently lead make customers feel safe.

The year Gerstad Builders won both the Avid Diamond Award and the Avid Cup, its president, Roger O. Gerstad, said his company elicited trust by having open dialogue with buyers: "We always wanted to be attentive...and build a home for each customer."[14] When we focus on customers and their needs over the homes themselves, we build an intimate, mutually beneficial relationship with our buyers.

As builder representatives, we must establish and maintain omakase with customers by demonstrating they can place their trust in us. Keeping customers well-informed is key to maintaining an environment where they feel comfortable leaving it to us.

3) Treat the person, not the disease.

In the movie *Patch Adams*, the title character says, "If you treat the disease, you win and you lose. If you treat the person, I guarantee, you win every time." When we recognize the cause and effect, and dig deeper into why we lose customers' confidence, we find the key to creating the best customer experience. It's about treating the deeper root, rather than the concern of the moment, and taking responsibility for the experience we are providing. Here's a big key: Customer service isn't the customer's issue.

If you don't like the effect, examine the cause.

Nervous customers may suddenly start complaining constantly. But while they rant about the carpet, they may just be nervous about the huge life change ahead. Or they may simply need some reassurance that you still care about them.

To illustrate, consider a common scenario with superintendents who are frustrated with how customers approach the walk-through. Builder representatives often don't consider how they can set expectations up front. Customers follow our lead. They feel they have to be on guard and come in with a magnifying glass, because if they don't spot every problem that day, they fear they're going to have to live with a less than perfect home.

Are you ready for a gut check? The housing industry has trained customers to see the walk-through as a gripe session. It's well past time to stop pointing fingers and understand that customers see it that way because of how homebuilders have set it up.

To retrain customers, keep the approach positive. Set buyers up to learn about their new home with language like, "Join us for an exciting session: The delivery of your new home!" Present it like a brand-new car and show off all its bells and whistles instead of treating it like an Easter egg hunt for problems. This is how we address the cause of the effect we don't like. This is what it means to treat the disease.

Customer intimacy is like a drug. While we are actively tending to customers, we bolster them with reassurance that they are making the right decision. Sadly, when they need reassurance most (after signing), we often shift our attention and stop providing it for them. Our disinterest and lack of communication causes their uncertainty. And when certainty is lost, all is lost.

When certainty is lost, all is lost.

When we realize our behavior causes their anxiety, we can shift our mindset and our behaviors. If we remember that often when customers arrive with concerns they are just craving reassurance, we'll handle the situation differently.

~

Customer intimacy exists when homebuyers that not only believe they've made the right decision, but that their builder, salesperson, superintendent, and all other company representatives are competent, trustworthy, and on their side.

Customer service is easy. It's psychology that gets in the way.

By being empathetic, building trust, and recognizing your role in difficult buyer behaviors, you will forge deeper connections. Better yet, the more security and intimacy customers have, the more willing they will be to tolerate hiccups in the process. When we build customer intimacy, issues often suddenly disappear. Commit to this approach and you'll build unbreakable customer certainty.

[12] Katherine Harmon, "How Important Is Physical Contact with Your Infant?" *Scientific American*, May 6, 2010, http://www.scientificamerican.com/article/infant-touch/.

[13] "Man who shot Pope John Paul II visits his tomb," *CBS News*, December 27, 2014, http://www.cbsnews.com/news/man-who-shot-pope-john-paul-ii-visits-his-tomb/.

[14] Paul Cardis, "2008 Avid Awards: Gerstad Builders," *Professional Builder*, November 1, 2008, http://www.probuilder.com/2008-avid-awards-gerstad-builders.

BEST PRACTICE 6
Bust the Service Myths or the Myths Will Bust You

"Half a truth is often a great lie."
-Benjamin Franklin

THE 4 HARMFUL CUSTOMER SERVICE MYTHS

THE CUSTOMER
IS ALWAYS RIGHT

1

ONLY UNHAPPY
CUSTOMERS FILL
OUT SURVEYS

2

CUSTOMERS KNOW
WHAT THEY WANT

3

CUSTOMERS WILL
ALWAYS TELL YOU WHEN
THEY'RE UNHAPPY

4

"Builders often come to Avid insisting they have to have higher survey response rates in order to feel the results truly represent the big picture. But study after study proves this myth untrue. We drive response rates up to 70% and every time, we find there's only a negligible difference (<1%) in results. It's a myth that causes builders extra headaches. You don't have to eat the whole pie to know what the pie tastes like."

—Paul

Lightning never strikes the same place twice—or so we mistakenly believe. Turns out the opposite is actually true. NASA dispelled this myth in 2003,[15] showing that places previously struck by lightning are statistically more likely to be struck again.[16] But we are still catching up with the times. Knowing the truth can save lives and propel people to get out of harm's way.

Homebuilding myths might not get you struck by lightning, but getting at the truth positions builders to better create service certainty for each customer. The following four customer service myths are particularly harmful to business:

Myth 1: The customer is always right.

Kids are masters of persuasion. They work their parents to get what they want, and they quickly learn that one parent's "no" doesn't mean all hope is lost. If Mom draws a line, they may ask Dad. But even when they get the answer they're looking for, they feel insecure because their parents are not on the same page. They think they want a green light, but what they really want is the security that their parents are united and will set boundaries to keep them safe.

Like children, customers see through and exploit our insecurities. However, while they may think they want a "yes" to all their requests, they actually want to feel like they can trust their builder and its employees. When company representatives knock the builder's processes or policies by saying, "If I were in charge, we would do things differently," it creates distrust. Though it may not feel good to them at first, customers feel settled when builder representatives reinforce company policies.

It can be a big shock when the homebuyers we invest the most time in and bend over backwards for are the ones who give the worst feedback. This stems from the biggest myth about customer experience: the customer is always right. By agreeing to everything customers ask for, company representatives actually contribute to uncertainty, rather than leading customers through the process in a way that shows we have the experience to know better than they do.

From construction to financing, and everything in between, employees must be assertive and confident in order to build trust with buyers. Operating as a team and presenting a united front builds customer certainty.

 A common myth in customer satisfaction is that you need to have at least 75% of your customers taking your survey.

Myth 2: Only unhappy customers fill out surveys.

We've all heard that "angry buyers speak the loudest," but it's not true. Avid gets the highest response rates from the happiest customers. The second highest response rate does indeed come from the unhappy customers, though, demonstrating that angry buyers do want to make their voices heard.

Here's why it's important not to believe the myth that you'll only hear the angry voices: It makes it easy to discount the results rather than attempting to improve. If you think you're only hearing from outliers, it's tempting to blame the response rate (not your performance), or to be frustrated enough by customer feedback to engage in review fraud and review scrubbing. The only thing worse than not asking for feedback is asking for feedback and not paying attention to it. Why spend all that money and effort just to ignore the findings?

Our opening story speaks to this myth. The truth is that Avid's lowest response rates (which come from moderately performing builders) are still accurate, and attempts to increase response rates produce little change in results. In 2015, Avid received an overall 59% response rate across its entire database of clients—plenty to accurately measure real performance.

AVID RATINGS STUDY, 2013

Avid Ratings surveyed over 400 customers on a 30-day homebuyer survey.

 At the 50% response mark, they analyzed the data.

They then sent out a survey reminder to the remaining customers and waited.

At the 75% response mark, they analyzed the data again.

FROM 50% TO 75%, THE HOMEBUYER SURVEY CHANGED LESS THAN 1 POINT, WHICH IS NOT STATISTICALLY SIGNIFICANT.

Myth 3: Customers know what they want.

Steve Jobs didn't want focus groups and research to tell him what people wanted. Instead, he created products consumers didn't even know were possible and then made it so people couldn't live without them. People didn't realize a powerful computer could one day fit in their pockets, for example, but now feel naked without their smartphones. Another example is indoor plumbing. What was out-of-this-world amazing in the 1920s is now a standard feature nearly all people in our culture would never choose to live without.

Customers do know some of what they want. They always walk through the door with strong opinions about something. But the Kano model (a theory developed in the 1980s to identify customer needs) divides the world into wows, wants, and must haves.[17] The wows are things people don't realize they want, but are delighted by. When we deliver these, we create a whole new level of certainty.

We have to think beyond what customers tell us they want. The danger of this myth is that if you follow what customers tell you, you risk under-delivering. In order to be memorable and increase loyalty among buyers, you must exceed expectations and deliver the wows.

Myth 4: Customers will always tell you when they're unhappy.

There's a widespread phenomenon that happens with a mediocre meal at a restaurant. You may have just told your companion that you were disappointed with your dinner, but when a server or manager asks how everything is, you say, "It's fine."

Unless it's really bad, we rarely tell the truth. We take the easy way out. This phenomenon is called the *social desirability bias* and refers to the error in self-report surveys due to the desire to paint ourselves in the best light possible and also avoid conflict.[18]

Like the customer, the manager or server surely knows not every meal is up to par. But they take the easy way out, too. Instead of digging deeper, or using third-party research, they just take your word for it and move on.

This means having salespeople solicit customer feedback isn't enough. The results aren't accurate. The question "Do you have anything we need to talk about?" will nearly always get a "No." It's a dummy call people do to check off the list, but it doesn't actually accomplish anything. This is why it's so important for third-party researchers to dig deeper to find the truth, build rapport, and provide a forum so customers feel comfortable bringing up concerns.

~

Believing prominent myths is easy because they are so often repeated. But these beliefs hinder you and your customers. We're better off living in reality than taking the easy way out or skipping surveys that can give us a true understanding of our customers' experience.

It's time to be myth busters instead of myth followers.

[15] NASA, "Lightning Really Does Strike More Than Twice," *NASA*, January 13, 2003, http://www.nasa.gov/centers/goddard/news/topstory/2003/0107lightning.html.

[16] "Severe Weather 101 - Lightning," *National Severe Storms Laboratory*, accessed June 19, 2016, http://www.nssl.noaa.gov/education/svrwx101/lightning/faq/.

[17] "Kano Model Tutorial," *ASQ*, accessed February 4, 2016, http://asq.org/learn-about-quality/qfd-quality-function-deployment/overview/kano-model.html.

[18] R. J. Fisher, "Social Desirability Bias and the Validity of Indirect Questioning," *Journal of Consumer Research*, 20 (1993) 303-315, https://www.mendeley.com/catalog/social-indirect-desirability-questioning-bias-validity/.

BEST PRACTICE 7

Lead Customers or They Will Leave You

"A leader is one who knows the way, goes the way, and shows the way."
-John C. Maxwell

THE 2 KEY STEPS TO LEADING AND KEEPING YOUR CUSTOMERS

REMEMBER WHO
THE EXPERT IS **1**

DETERMINE THE FLOW, **2**
PACE, AND DIRECTION
OF EACH VISIT

"I used to file taxes myself, spending hours upon hours and giving myself head-aches each tax season researching rules. I just didn't see the value in paying someone else until an accountant could prove he was worth the cost. When I felt I could hand the whole process over and get on with my life, I gladly paid. As long as I can trust my tax advisers to be the gurus, they're worth every penny."

—Jason

While we're myth busting, let's dispel one of the most prominent of all: customers want to lead the process. This one is so damaging it deserves its own best practice. If you were to ask potential buyers if they want to be in charge, they would likely say yes. But it's just not true. In reality, customers want and need builder representatives to lead. They need our expertise and are grateful to get it. When we view ourselves as facilitators rather than leaders, we hold back, delay delivering bad news, or avoid difficult conversations because we are afraid of coming across as pushy or self-serving. While we may think we're doing right by our customers, we're not doing anybody any favors.

As always, we must change the way we think. When people lack expertise in certain areas, they want to follow a leader. Customers want to know their company representatives know the process inside and out and care about finding the best solution to their issues. They want and need a strong and consistent leader. As builder representatives, we're the ones who have done this before. We know what we're doing and must step into our leadership roles.

Be a leader they want to follow

Follow two key steps to lead (and keep) your customers:

1) Remember who the expert is.

Seinfeld fans will remember the tyrannical Soup Nazi—the character who imposed ridiculous orders on customers. If they didn't comply, he refused them service, barking, "No soup for you!" The character is inspired by real-life Ali Yeganeh, who owns a soup restaurant in New York City and is infamous for his strict rules about how customers wait in line, pay, and even order his soup. Ali runs the show.[19]

The customer isn't responsible for driving the customer experience—we are. Obviously it's not about being rude and kicking customers out of your line, but if you acquiesce to every single demand of the customer, you won't be able to create a consistent and delightful customer experience.

Customers want company representatives to lead.

Particularly in our industry, customers spend endless hours online researching neighborhoods, appliances, mortgage rates, and more. All that time staring at a screen is exhausting. Whether they are designing their home or watching it being built, customers feel they are in good hands when builder representatives demonstrate authority and lead. They don't want to have to figure it all out on their own. They don't need to know everything about the building process. Instead, they need to know you know. When they are confident you have everything under control, it takes off pressure. Leadership builds certainty.

Leadership removes pressure and builds certainty.

As the company representative, be the expert, and make it your goal to provide value that is greater than the paycheck you will earn and the money they are paying. Customers will be relieved to have found a human Google in their knowledgeable company representative. To find solutions, act like a detective—uncovering clues about what will improve each customer's situation. You almost certainly know options and solutions they are unaware of.

2) Determine the flow, pace, and direction of each visit.

As the leader in the relationship, company representatives must determine the flow, pace, and direction of each visit. We're not advocating being an overbearing jerk or doing all the talking. It's the opposite. Ask the right questions and truly listen to and understand their responses. Anticipate customers' needs and lead them to solutions for their unique problems. Identify the right destination and walk them towards it.

Customers come to us for support in doing something they can't do on their own, and we are the ones who can help them reach their goal. To establish yourself as a leader, talk about what comes next every time you're with them. Say, "Here's what we are doing now. Here's why we are going to do it. Once we accomplish this, we'll talk about what's next." This shows you know what's coming and gives you credibility.

~

Holding back information, advice, and opinions doesn't benefit customers. Have some courage and facilitate the journey. Over-communicate. Make it as easy as possible on your customers so they don't have to babysit the process. They, in turn, will feel safe, confident, and certain in their decision. We don't want to pay someone to do our taxes while still feeling like we need to have our hands in the whole thing.

If we let customers take the lead, we get left behind—and they lose out on getting the best experience. Customers have ideas and dreams (but often without the experience to know how to reach their desired destinations). As builder representatives, we are best equipped to lead them to the solution they desire. When we think of ourselves as leaders and we lead with confidence, we create customer certainty. When we lead, everyone wins.

[19] Miss Cellania, "The Real Life Soup Nazi," *Neatorama,* May 15, 2014, http://www.neatorama.com/2014/05/15/The-Real-Life-Soup-Nazi/.

BEST PRACTICE 8
Make Yourself Unleavable

"Make a customer, not a sale."
-Katherine Barchetti

THE 3 STEPS TO MAKING YOURSELF UNLEAVABLE

CARE MORE ABOUT THE CUSTOMER THAN THE CONTRACT **1**

CREATE A HOME THEY LOVE, NOT HANDCUFFS THAT TRAP THEM **2**

MAKE CUSTOMERS FEEL IMPORTANT **3**

"There's a large North American home manufacturer that demonstrates the arrogance of the homebuilding industry perfectly. They post rules on the door that ensure customers enter their homes with maximum discomfort and insecurity. Their condescending, bulleted list treats customers like an inconvenience. It tells parents to keep kids under control (including no jumping on beds) and requires all customers to remove footwear and leave snacks in the car. It provokes me something fierce."

—Jason

Homebuilding is one of the only industries that gets away with being jerks. This means customers end up in a "have to" (unfireable) mode instead of a "want to" (unleavable) situation. Fear motivates "have to" situations—just like going to the dentist. It's something we do begrudgingly because we're afraid all of our teeth will fall out of our face if we don't. On the flip side, love and certainty motivate customers in a "want to" situation.

If your favorite grocery store had a sign saying: "Please remove your dirty shoes before entering," you would turn around and drive to the next store. Yet builders—especially during a seller's market—believe everyone should cater to their needs.

Make customers feel important.

Customers, who arrive excited about the possibilities for their future, feel slammed before the salesperson even has a chance to say hello. If they are insecure about their kids' behavior, how can we expect them to fall in love with the solution we're presenting? Or, if they've spent the morning driving all over town, they may turn around at the door rather than require hungry kids to throw away their snacks and drinks. And we wonder why homebuyers' walls are up throughout the entire buying/building experience? Just as dogs bite back when they're afraid, people become cool and cynical if we start the relationship on the wrong foot or arrogantly assume their business is ours for the taking. When we have customers yelling at us for being the Big Bad Builder, we have to consider whether we have created a defensive relationship.

Follow these three steps to make yourself unleavable:

1) Care more about the customer than the contract.

Jason's friends John and Shannon are in the middle of a miserable home buying experience. They have little confidence in their builder and feel they have to micromanage the process. They want to cancel, but between their earnest money deposit and the time and money they've invested in architectural plans and more, they feel stuck. It's a crappy way to buy what should be their dream home. Their builder does not have their loyalty or certainty but has become, in their view, unfireable.

The contract includes a clause that if the house takes too long and material prices increase, John and Shannon will be on the hook for the additional costs. They've heard the classic line, "You signed off on the contract so there's nothing you can do about it," more times than they care to count.

If all you strive for is not being fired, you're taking a losing strategy.

Even though it's in every other room in the house, the builder didn't include crown molding in the game room. They were told, "Technically yes, you should have molding. But it will be an upgrade if you decide to add it because you signed off on the initial bid." This approach penalizes them for trusting the builder to cover such details. It's the builder's mistake, but because John and Shannon didn't see it in the encyclopedia-length contract, they're stuck. This is what we mean about the builder being unfireable. John and Shannon feel trapped. The devil is in the details. Stay on top of those and you'll look like an angel.

2) Create a home they love, not handcuffs that trap them.

Big earnest money deposits allow builders to hedge their bets against cancellations, but also essentially trap the consumer. If your goal is just to get them to not cancel, mission accomplished. But if your goal is to create addicted fans, then it's a counterproductive approach. Low cancellation rates don't automatically mean happy customers.

Builders, salespeople, superintendents, and warranty reps can't stand angry buyers...yet sometimes they are inviting their own misery. If each time John and Shannon walk through the sales office doors, it is with dread and cynicism, it makes the relationship extra challenging.

Of course, we understand it from the company's point of view, too. It costs a ton of money to build a house for someone who cancels, and reselling a customized home is challenging. But holding customers hostage is not the right way to keep them. It's our job to treat them right and do our best to create a situation where buyers are so happy with us they simply wouldn't dream of leaving, even when problems arise.

This is going to be their home. We don't always have to say yes, but when we treat customer requests as though they are as important as our own desires, homebuyers have a much harder time walking away—not because they have money on the line, but because builder representatives have earned their trust and loyalty.

3) Make customers feel important.

Let's go back to our example of the builder who imposes a list of restrictions on visitors as soon as they walk in. Imagine if that sign said something like: "We're so glad you're here and we hope you enjoy your visit. Our home is your home." Imagine if tired, hungry families walked through the door to a bowl of snacks and a refrigerator full of drinks. What if we made their experience more like visiting the Ritz-Carlton than going through an airport security line?

Making a few simple changes dramatically transforms the customer's experience and makes the builder stand apart from industry norms. It's a simple solution: Examine everything you do in the company and see if it creates trust or traps buyers. Change is possible. With a mindset shift, your company can earn a new reputation as the go-to builder.

Take the Mary Kay approach and pretend all customers have signs around their neck saying: "Make me feel important." This is what makes a company stand out in a positive way—as the only builder who lets kids be kids, for example.

~

At Avid and FPG, we strive to run our businesses in a way that makes us unleavable. If we wanted to be unfireable, we'd get the biggest, baddest attorneys to draw up ironclad contracts. When problems arose, we'd say, "You've already signed." Instead, we work our butts off to provide so much value that clients justify the expense, knowing our service is worth more than they pay. If we're not providing the value that makes us impossible to leave, we see it as our own fault.

The way many builders treat customers is counterproductive and leads to a compromised brand. It's bad business and hurts both the customer and the company. Instead of posting signs dictating what future homeowners can and cannot do in our models or using their earnest money and time invested to handcuff them when the building process becomes difficult, give them an unbeatable experience. Every step of the buying process should be as positive as possible.

One thing that deflates our arrogance faster than the 2007 housing bubble is remembering the economy is always, always, always cyclical. We may have buyers lining up at our door one season but be forced to endure layoffs the next. When it shifts to a buyer's market, we can get away with less. But even when we can get away with bad behavior, we should treat people right. Always.

Builders are not above the rules of common courtesy. So let's drop the arrogance and look for opportunities to provide a standout experience. Make the customer feel like gold instead of being the Big Bad Builder who threatens to blow their house down.

BEST PRACTICE 9
Close the Procrastination Gap

"Life has no limitations,
except the ones you make."
-Les Brown

THE 3 STEPS TO STRENGTHEN MOTIVATION

REKINDLE CUSTOMERS' VISION/REASONS FOR BUYING **1**

OVERCOME LIMITING BELIEFS **2**

GET THEM TO STATE THEIR INTENTIONS ALOUD **3**

"When I was dragging my feet on having a difficult conversation with an employee, my executive coach, Catherine Crosslin, said, 'You are procrastinating either because you don't have a strong enough vision [motivation] or your beliefs are limiting you.'"

—Jason

Whether your goal is to get in shape, make a career change, or buy a new home, there is often a gap between the destination and your current situation. That gap may be filled with procrastination, fear, limited resources, a lack of experience/training, or any number of obstacles. When procrastination or fear fill that gap, there is one main reason: the perceived obstacles are stronger than the motivation to reach the goal. When homebuyers stall at any point in the process, company representatives must move them forward by addressing their false beliefs and getting them to state their needs out loud (thereby strengthening their motivation).

Overcome limiting beliefs and strengthen motivation with these three steps:

1) Rekindle customers' vision/reasons for buying.

To illustrate, we'll talk about one example that can instantly make customers drag their feet: the mortgage qualification process. Money issues tend to have a BIG stigma attached to them. It can feel like judgment day to go through each line of your credit report with a loan officer who can either move your purchase forward or end your dream with the stroke of a pen or a click of the mouse. Even when homebuyers find their ideal home, misgivings about this process can be enough to keep them from taking the necessary steps to improve their lives. The motivation needs to outpace the fear of judgment day. This is where company representatives come in.

Alleviate the "judgment day" mentality around finances.

Whatever the situation, builder representatives must find out what's compelling customers forward, what's holding them back, and how to close the gap. Homebuyers may procrastinate by not attending required appointments, not signing paperwork, not working with the lender, rescheduling construction appointments, putting off design selections, and so on. By not coming to a final conclusion, they're deliberately (even if subconsciously) delaying the process.

But if you can find out why they want to buy and what the reward is on the other end, you can motivate them to move forward. It may be about giving their kids a better future or a safer environment. It might be the backyard that's just perfect for their dream garden. They may be trying to prove to themselves, or others, that they can do it, or find security and establish roots. Discover their "why" to rekindle their motivation.

Remove self-inflicted uncertainty.

2) Overcome limiting beliefs.

If customers aren't moving forward despite all their compelling reasons, limiting beliefs are holding them back. Maybe they think they can't afford to buy or are afraid to even try to find out. Or maybe they feel they don't have time or it's going to be too much work. Whatever it is, find out. This knowledge will be a valuable tool in leading them forward and making them feel secure and certain.

Talk through each concern and give examples of people in similar situations who have overcome the same roadblocks. The irony is that they are unhappy in their current situation but unable to move forward. You will be a hero to them if you lead them to overcome the beliefs that are leading to their self-inflicted dissatisfaction.

3) Get them to state their intentions aloud.

An important step in closing the gap is to get people to state their needs and intentions aloud. Think about the last time you shared a goal with someone. Maybe you wanted to write a book, climb a mountain, or improve your health. As long as it's a private desire, you can talk yourself out of it. You can convince yourself it's too hard or will take too long. Once you say it aloud, though, it gets real and your confidant can provide accountability.

Think about what happens when people realize they've met their future spouse. The possibility instantly rises to a whole new level once they admit it to a friend or family member. The more they share their intentions, the more powerful and meaningful these intentions become. Once customers admit a goal (to you, their spouse, the stranger at the gas station), the motivation becomes personal.

~

Buyers who have every reason to move forward in the sale or design process, but who lack urgency are stuck. Remove the limiting beliefs and lead them to share their compelling reasons for moving forward. Be the hero who changes fear into progress.

BEST PRACTICE 10

Be an Adviser to Increase Customer Commitment

"A leader takes people where they want to go. A great leader takes people where they don't necessarily want to go, but ought to be."

- Rosalynn Carter

THE 4 STEPS TO BECOMING AN ADVISER AND INCREASING CUSTOMER COMMITMENT

COMMUNICATE 1

CHALLENGE PERSPECTIVES 2

LEAD THE COMPROMISE 3

COLLABORATE 4

"'Your number one priority should not be your customer.' It was a line I knew would either have my prospect signing on the dotted line or walking me out the door. I was telling a potential client (already the second most successful car sales company in the country) that their focus was wrong. While they insisted their success hinged on their 'customer first' approach, I told them their top priority needed to be themselves. Braman Motorcars had gotten to second in the nation with their focus, but they were stuck. They wanted to grow and I explained that when their own culture was in line, their customers would naturally be taken care of. This is when I became their adviser and got the training contract."

—Jason

When customers see company representatives as advisers, certainty increases. They can find a vendor (someone who sells a replaceable commodity) anywhere, but a trusted adviser is hard to replace. Becoming an adviser goes hand-in-hand with creating service certainty because it ensures you understand their mission and are on their team to make it happen.

Below are four steps to becoming an adviser and increasing customer commitment:

1) Communicate.

Good internal communication is crucial to building customer certainty. Remember Jason's friends John and Shannon? They see their builder as a vendor in part because of poor internal communication between the superintendent and the office. For example, when John went to the superintendent with a picture of a shower they'd gotten approved through the office, he discovered that the super didn't know anything about it. Since the super wasn't in the loop, John and Shannon saw him as a vendor. Certainty requires company representatives to communicate with purpose. Advisers communicate with confidence and direction, building trust with every move.

2) Challenge perspectives.

Challenging in a good, assertive way solidifies your place as an adviser. It's about changing the way customers look at things. When a customer asks, "Why didn't we do it this way?" advisers help them understand the builder's perspective. For example, when customers complain about small lots, the builder representative might say, "In order to build affordable homes in this terrific school district, we had to make the lot sizes smaller." Challenging perspectives makes us advisers. If we can't help customers see things differently, why do they need us?

3) Lead the compromise.

Despite your experience, sometimes customers think they know better. You can't be afraid to lead them to a solution. Consider the above example further. A customer who wants large lots, the best school district, and low prices may have to decide which of those is a must-have and which they can do without. Have the courage to tell them what they need to hear, and remember that it's better for them in the long run.

Involve customers in coming up with their own solutions. Ask questions and sincerely listen to their responses. You may know something won't work, but instead of putting them on the defense by saying, "No, that isn't the right direction for you," allow them to be a part of the decision. Become partners in the solution by providing a choice. This allows you to identify the right destination and lead them toward it.

4) Collaborate.

If builder representatives challenge and force the compromise without including collaboration, they may end up with the result they want, but the customer won't feel good about it. The only thing worse than a company representative unwilling to lead is one who dictates. This is no way to build a business. Advisers must also be collaborators because collaboration builds loyalty and makes customers feel proud of their decisions. We defend what we create.

~

By communicating, advice confidently, facilitating compromise, and collaborating, you will create certainty and earn a reputation as an adviser (along with its corresponding success). Without your advisership, customers will never be fully committed. If you do it right, though, you'll create increased commitment and customer loyalty.

BEST PRACTICE 11
Practice Service Recovery

"Customers don't expect you to be perfect. They do expect you to fix things when they go wrong."
-Donald Porter

THE 8 STEPS TO TURN ANGRY BUYERS INTO LOYAL FANS

ACKNOWLEDGE THEIR ANGER **1**

LISTEN CAREFULLY **2**

KEEP YOUR COOL **3**

PROBE **4**

BE EMPATHETIC **5**

SEEK THEIR SOLUTIONS **6**

TAKE ACTION **7**

FOLLOW UP **8**

"In 2004, every room in my new home was filled with house guests...and every bathroom drain was filled with backed-up sewage. The connection to the main sewer was severely blocked with construction debris, and the resulting warranty issue had the potential to become a major sore spot between the builder and us. Instead, company representatives responded quickly and even put all my guests up at a nearby hotel while they dug up the street, removed the blockage, and cleaned up the house. Because the builder responded swiftly and confidently to a bad situation, they earned my loyalty—why would I trust anyone else when they did such a good job?"

—Paul

Customer service is the cornerstone upon which successful businesses are built. Even if we provide exemplary service when circumstances beyond our control aggravate buyers, it's still our job to patch injured relationships. For example, when delivery schedules get behind due to poor weather, little can be done to change the situation. What you can do is consider the customer's perspective and do everything within reason to turn potentially damaging situations into loyalty-building opportunities.

One or two angry customers might not seem detrimental, but damage to a reputation and business can quickly build.

These customers will be looking for some gesture of atonement or compensation. If the service hasn't met their expectations, they need service recovery. Effective service recovery should be specific to the situation and personal so it doesn't appear you're doing something just to get rid of an angry customer.

Renew your customer's faith in the relationship.

In *Knock Your Socks Off Service Recovery*, Chip Bell explains what happens when you fail to meet customer expectations and they're left psychologically and emotionally disappointed. According to Bell, customers come with certain expectations in mind, which may or may not be in line with what you can deliver. If those expectations aren't met, they feel betrayed. To regain the customer's confidence, communicate in a way that will renew their faith in the relationship.[20]

Many builder representatives are reluctant to apologize for fear they will be admitting to some liability or expressing weakness, but a genuine apology is usually the first and most powerful step in repairing the damage. Taking responsibility and making things right reestablishes trust. When angry customers confront, they are looking for an authentic demonstration of humility.

Eight simple (though not easy) steps can turn angry buyers into loyal fans:

1) **Acknowledge their anger:** Nothing enrages customers more than feeling ignored or trivialized. The faster the acknowledgment, the easier the situation will be to resolve.

2) **Listen carefully:** While hearing complaints, take notes to show you care and are taking the matter seriously. Don't try to rush customers; instead, give them time to vent and say everything they want. Don't interrupt. Customers will often cool off and realize they blew things out of proportion.

3) **Keep your cool:** Angry people often utter things they don't really mean. Don't take it personally. Respond in a calm manner and stay focused on the issue at hand.

4) Probe: Ask questions to make sure you understand the real problem and source of the anger. Through careful questioning, you will be better prepared to offer meaningful solutions.

5) Be empathetic: Identifying with your customer's plight doesn't necessarily mean you can feel his or her pain; it simply means you can appreciate the inconvenience, trouble, stress, etc. the problem has caused. Upset customers want to know two things: that you care about them personally and that you're going to do something to remedy the situation.

Consider the customer's perspective.

6) Seek their solutions: Once customers are calm, ask what they'd like you to do. Often, their proposal will cost you less than what you would have suggested while making them feel validated—it's a win/win! If the demand is unreasonable, ask the homebuyer to explain their rationale. If there's a clear misunderstanding about a product or service, give the buyer the benefit of the doubt. If you've tried to be receptive and the client is still irate, explain that you'd like some time to work on a solution, and schedule another meeting. By then the customer will likely be calm.

7) Take action: Propose a specific and quick solution that both parties can agree on, and put it in writing. Agree on a specific timeframe for accomplishing what you say you'll do. Then do it. During this period, keep the customer informed. If you run into a snag and need to alter your agreement, be open and honest and consult with the homebuyer right away.

8) Follow up: Check in to make sure things are going well. Let customers know they were instrumental in bringing about changes that will help other homebuyers. If that's not true, you might say, "We haven't solved the problem that caused your situation, but we're working on it." This shows you're sincerely concerned about what happened to them.

~

Customers who have their complaints successfully resolved often become more loyal. From their perspective, they've seen you screw up and they've seen how you sincerely care about them and want to resolve the situation. You don't have to build the perfect house, but you do have to handle challenges in a way that increases confidence, loyalty, and certainty.

Once you've resolved the situation satisfactorily, you'll have earned another opportunity to serve them in the future—and they'll tell their friends and family how well you handled a potentially disastrous situation. When you practice service recovery, you transform heartbreak into certainty and restore confidence in the relationship.

[20] Chip Bell and Ron Zemke, *Knock Your Socks Off Service Recovery*, (New York: AMACOM, 2000).

BEST PRACTICE 12
Call in the SWAT Team

"To be prepared for war is one of the most effective means of preserving peace."
-George Washington

THE 4 KEY STEPS TO BUILDING & UTILIZING A SWAT TEAM

IDENTIFY POTENTIALLY HOSTILE CUSTOMERS IN ADVANCE **1**

BUILD YOUR SWAT TEAM **2**

DOCUMENT ALL ACTIONS **3**

PROVIDE IMMEDIATE FOLLOW-UP AND RESOLUTION **4**

"With so many details, a lot can go wrong in homebuilding. One builder contacted me about an unresolved situation with an angry buyer. Although the buyer had originally moved into the home thinking everything was okay, he later started posting negative comments on Facebook. He included pictures of the home and its supposed defects—but these were actually photos from the walk-through and had been corrected before he moved in. His hostile behavior was shutting down sales and compromising the company's reputation.

Our team recommended meeting with the buyer and including the company's owner, which made quite an impression on the buyer. He was immediately disarmed when he realized the top dog cared about his concern. After the first meeting, the homeowner agreed to stop posting. Although the buyer initially wanted a cash buyout, they worked through the issues and came to a more reasonable solution. They reestablished the psychological respect, trust, and certainty that had been lost."

—Paul

Re-establish trust.

Special Weapons And Tactics (SWAT) is a division of many police forces specially trained to handle the most extreme situations. In day-to-day customer encounters, service recovery is an excellent strategy, but in the most extreme cases, when we've tried service recovery and customers still feel they are at war with builders, we need a much more aggressive strategy to stabilize the situation and potentially turn the toughest critics into the biggest fans.

Having an in-house SWAT team serves builders well. Difficult customers bring the emotion of all the hopes and dreams they have tied up in their home into the discussion. When they feel their dreams are threatened, only the most aggressive approach will ease their minds.

Every builder will benefit from a crew ready to go into action when a potentially hostile situation emerges. The toughest customers require special care. And it's worth it. According to the Avid database across thousands of homebuilders, leading builders who take a comprehensive customer approach have been able to reduce their percentage of hostile customers to less than one percent, while the rest of the industry has on average seven times more disgruntled customers.[21] Working with the toughest customers can yield tremendous return on investment.

Extreme cases require an extreme plan.

Not everyone immediately agrees, however. At a Homebuilders' Association event, one prominent consultant argued that homebuilders should not focus on satisfying their toughest customers. Instead, she argued, builders should devote their resources to making happy customers happier. Her rationale was that it's too difficult to turn disgruntled homebuyers into loyal advocates and more fruitful to turn moderately happy customers into ecstatic ones.

This simplistic view ignores the fact that we live in a digitally connected world, and companies have the power to recover the toughest buyers. It is critical for all companies to engage in this conflict resolution to maintain their brand as well as their bottom line. Homebuilding is a local business, and it doesn't take much to tarnish one's reputation and kill future sales. In 2007, Sprint Nextel publicly "fired" (dropped) its most difficult customers, angering subscribers and igniting a social media backlash.[22] In the subsequent years, Sprint Nextel hit troubled times as it lost millions of customers and faced dropping revenue.[23] This example, although drastic, exemplifies the need to make a proper recovery plan for difficult customers, rather than just writing them off. The silver lining for Sprint Nextel was a remarkable recovery over the following decade plus, which Gerardo Dada, in a blog post for Bazaarvoice, attributes to its shift toward customer centricity.[24]

Create an aggressive fix-it strategy to avoid getting burned.

Below are four key steps to building and utilizing a SWAT Team.

1) Identify potentially hostile customers in advance.

Have active CRM (customer relationship management) programs in place to identify buyers who may need intervention. The CRM program manages workflow and documents warranty requests, as well as the customer's history and touchpoints.

In addition to CRMs, third-party CSS (customer satisfaction survey) programs allow teams to properly assess performance (absent of bias), flag low scores, scan the internet for public reviews, and read comments to identify potentially hostile situations. Through examining data and obtaining knowledge of the customer's experience, the team can determine the status and address issues before they explode.

2) Build your SWAT team.

Your SWAT team should include a project superintendent, a warranty representative, and an executive from the main office who is authorized to make warranty repair decisions. The key is to assemble a team that will show homebuyers you take their concerns seriously. Also, by involving top-level personnel, the SWAT team will be able to offer solutions and quickly resolve matters without needing additional approval.

3) Document all actions.

The team should meet with the homebuyer at the house, which might require evening or weekend appointments, address each area of concern, and determine an appropriate fix. It helps if SWAT team members can empathize with homeowners and ask, "What would I expect the homebuilder to do if this were my house?" Document all discussions and actions for future reference.

Turn critics into addicts.

4) Provide immediate follow-up and resolution.

Track all issues and action plans to reach resolutions in a timely fashion. Preemptively address further dissatisfaction by alerting customers to any delays they can expect with repairs and remedies. Finally, present the homebuyers with a service recovery gift that reminds them how much the company appreciates their business and how important the homebuyer/builder relationship is.

Just as police stations would be happy to never deploy their special forces, builders hope to keep SWAT teams in reserve. But when a situation calls for specialized experts to deal with irate or hostile customers, having a team prepared to spring into action is a valuable insurance policy that is far superior to turning a blind eye.

~

Instead of getting defensive in the face of conflict or writing off our toughest customers, we need to strategically appeal to both happy and unhappy customers. A customer management strategy that addresses only moderately happy customers is not just ill-advised; it's dangerous to a builder's long-term success. Clearly, builders should focus their service efforts on the areas of greatest opportunity, but they also must have a process for dealing with those severely dissatisfied customers who can create a public relations nightmare.

Avid Ratings' data suggests the typical builder can expect around 7.5 percent of their customers to make a negative referral.[25] That's why we are staunch advocates of neutralizing your toughest customers AND appealing to your happier customers. This is about more than keeping one buyer happy. It's about protecting future business, too.

[21] Paul Cardis, "Why it Pays for Homebuilders to Work with Their Toughest Customers," *Professional Builder*, July 1, 2008, http://www.probuilder.com/why-it-pays-homebuilders-work-their-toughest-customers.

[22] Alex Cohen, "Sprint Drops Customers Who Call for Help Too Often," *NPR*, July 11, 2007, http://www.npr.org/templates/story/story.php?storyId=11873017.

[23] Jenna Wortham, "For Sprint Nextel, a Drop in Customers and Earnings," *The New York Times*, February 19, 2009, http://www.nytimes.com/2009/02/20/technology//20sprint.html?_r=0.

[24] Gerardo Dada, "Customer Centricity as Sprint's Turnaround Strategy," *Bazaarvoice*, July 6, 2010, http://blog.bazaarvoice.com/2010/07/06/customer-centricity-as-sprints-turnaround-strategy/.

[25] Ibid.

BEST PRACTICE 13
Define Culture from the Inside Out

"Be a yardstick of quality. Some people aren't used to an environment where excellence is expected."

-Steve Jobs

THE 3 STEPS TO BUILDING CULTURE FROM THE INSIDE OUT

DEFINE THE STANDARD 1

BUILD A TEAM THAT
IS LOYAL TO THE
COMPANY'S BRAND 2

TREAT EMPLOYEES RIGHT 3

"After Richmond American Homes' Southern California division won our highest honor, I wanted to find out what made its division president, Leonard Miller, tick. They were doing something right and as a leader of service certainty, I wanted to know what keys he felt led to such delighted homebuyers. One point stood out above all others: Miller told me he checked every decision against the brand and strived to hold true to it through any circumstance."

—Paul

In the day-to-day crunch of meetings, calls, and deadlines, it is tempting to succumb to mediocrity—yet the results will also be mediocre. Defining and working out the culture requires hard work, a belief in the end result, and an uncompromising commitment to delivering service certainty from start to finish—building the brand from the inside out. When the internal culture is strong, the external expression (the brand) will be equally strong.

Follow these three steps to build culture from the inside out:

1) Define the standard.

When it comes to your brand, "You can't blink,"[26] says Leonard Miller, President of Richmond American's Southern California division, 2015's Avid Cup Award winner. This award, which honors those builders with the highest customer experience scores during the first year (rather than just the first 30 days) of homeownership, carries extra weight because a lot can go wrong in the first year. Having happy customers at the end of that period is a much stronger testament than having happy customers on closing day. Winning this award among those with the most comprehensive survey results in the industry means these companies are walking the walk.

Change the way you look at brand.

Brand is bigger than colors and slogans and is defined in customers' eyes every time the customer and any employee touch.[27] For Miller, it's bigger than taglines, which don't mean anything unless the standards are carried out with internal procedures and with each customer interaction—as well as in every financial situation and individual circumstance. Creating a culture of excellence requires absolute commitment to exceptional customer service and employees who understand and support the company's standards.

Every builder understands the pressure to close a certain number of homes at all costs, but final closing numbers don't reflect whether customers were disappointed or elated. In 2009, Miller drew the line in the sand and said they simply wouldn't close homes that didn't meet their quality standards. He believed this would lead to the best customer experience. Of course, anytime a leader or company makes that kind of declaration, much attention will be paid to see how the theory plays out in practice.

Shortly after making this brand commitment, the division faced its first test. With her moving truck packed and no backup plan in place, an older woman buying at a coastal community was desperate to get into her home. Unfortunately, as ready as she was, the flooring just wasn't done. She insisted she didn't care and had to move in on the weekend she planned. Miller thought, "I've been preaching this standard, but in this particular circumstance, I so want to make an exception." He called the buyer personally to talk her through it and stood his ground. The team was watching. Miller said, "Everybody was looking to see if I'd blink, but if you're not living it every day, you're not going to have that cultural value."[28] Miller holds maintaining the strength of the long-term culture as a higher goal than short-term, artificial payoffs.

2) Build a team that is loyal to the company's brand.

It's not enough to commit to exceptional customer service. We must also commit to building a team that believes in the company's brand enough to walk it out in daily circumstances. Beliefs drive behaviors. This mindset shift requires a team approach. If the brand is defined in the customer's eyes during every contact with each builder representative, then we all have a part in it—from sales to the design center to warranty and everywhere in between. It takes a team to build a dream.

In the movie *Braveheart*, Mel Gibson's character cries "Alba gu bràth!" as he and his men charge boldly into battle. The Gaelic phrase, which translates roughly to: "Scotland forever!" inspired the soldiers to remember why they were fighting. Creating a culture worth rallying around is useful in the battle of day-to-day business as well because it instills ownership in each person. This is how Miller led his division first to happy customers and then to awards and accolades.

Miller's commitment is a way of doing business that translates to an internal culture people can be proud of—one where employees are loyal to their peers, their leadership, and their company. Nobody wants to go to work every day when they aren't proud of their company.

> # When every employee is in line with the brand, customers get the best experience.

The only way to grab hold of the team's passion and get them to own the brand is to make sure they understand the why. There must be a compelling reason for employees to make the company's goals their own. Miller can't just say, "This is how we do it." He needs to be able to communicate why it's important—why it benefits the customer, the division, and the employee specifically.

Builders need each company representative's buy-in to achieve the goal. If the brand is defined by each employee's interaction with each customer, the whole division has to be in line. In Richmond's Southern California division, managers read every survey, and they go through each one together at their weekly operations meetings. Miller says, "The enthusiastic comments we get about certain [builder representatives] are far beyond the norm."[29] These positive responses demonstrate an intense customer loyalty. When problems pop up and patterns emerge from the comments, they discuss solutions. They also highlight positive comments by posting them on the walls. This brings everyone into the brand and gives each employee a personal reason to fight to maintain the standard.

When everyone knows what the company is doing and why, each person will be inspired to come up with their own personal ways to support the vision. We can't guarantee the results, but we can develop a strategy and get ownership from the team.

People like being part of a team that fights for goals and celebrates victories together. While team members at Richmond American Homes in Southern California probably have days they wish their division would bend, they are also likely proud to have the award they each share a part in. When each employee "owns" the culture that made the award possible, the reward truly is everyone's.

Building this kind of culture leads to better morale internally, and customers benefit too. Everyone is affected when the company wins or loses. If employees like coming to work, customers will feel it. Conversely, when morale is low or sales are weak, the whole team suffers. Building an internal culture of individual ownership and pride gives each member the opportunity to both develop and benefit from the company's growth.

3) Treat employees right.

The way employees feel about the company corresponds directly to the way they're treated. FPG and Avid Ratings share the philosophy that it's impossible to improve customer loyalty without improving employee engagement and loyalty (meaning employees are personally committed to supporting the organization's culture).

According to Gallup, engaged employees "feel a profound connection to their company" and bring extra effort to their work.[30] Without this connection to the company they work for, employees won't feel compelled to go the extra mile for customers. Rather than training employees to go the extra mile, companies truly benefit from investing in culture (so employees have something to feel connected and loyal to). Such a culture not only prevents employees from becoming disgruntled (and potentially damaging the company), but also builds a united team, where everyone does what it takes to ensure happy customers.

Unfortunately, there is a greater percentage of disloyal employees than loyal ones in America.[31] This startling trend has a significant impact on organizations, causing high turnover rates, low sales figures, and dissatisfied customers. A survey by Walker Information found that loyal employees are twice as likely as disloyal employees to execute company strategies in their daily work.[32] No matter how good the company strategies are, if employees at every level aren't committed to executing those strategies, they may as well not exist. The survey results continue: "Loyal employees are also more focused on helping the company succeed, and they are more willing to help colleagues with heavy workloads." Conversely, disgruntled employees are more likely to "cause significant damage to a company's reputation."[33] Be proactive and provide systems that value employees' contributions and acknowledge their concerns.

~

Builders focus too much on the how to (behaviors) of customer care and not enough on the beliefs and culture that lead to genuinely caring for customers. How employees treat customers is a direct result of how the employees feel about their job and their company. With an internal culture of trust, accountability, and leadership, people at every level provide exceptional customer care without being asked. A culture of excellence involves every person in the company and leads to addicted, raving fans.

With its many ups and downs, the housing industry is a tough one! Leaders who want teams to adopt the right beliefs must do one thing above all else: Demonstrate the beliefs they advocate. Miller says, "It comes down to walking the walk every day and having the right team."[34]

Make the brand so much a part of the culture that leaders and employees alike execute it in daily decisions—creating a culture that leads to delighted customers—from the inside out.

[26] In discussion with the author, Paul Cardis, May 28, 2015.

[27] Gallup, "Living the brand: Beyond T-shirts: The Case for Brand Talent," *Gallup Business Journal*, November 6, 2000. http://www.gallup.com/businessjournal/208/living-brand.aspx.

[28] In discussion with the author, Paul Cardis, May 28, 2015.

[29] Ibid.

[30] Gallup, "Five Ways to Improve Employee Engagement," *Gallup Business Journal*, January 7, 2014, http://www.gallup.com/businessjournal/166667/five-ways-improve-employee-engagement.aspx.

[31] Walker Information, "The Walker Loyalty Report for Loyalty in the Workplace," PDF file, 3, September 2007, http://www.walkerinfo.com/employeeloyalty/Employee_ExecSummary.pdf.

[32] Ibid.

[33] Ibid.

[34] In discussion with the author, Paul Cardis, May 28, 2015.

BEST PRACTICE 14
Do the Right Thing

"Initiative is doing the right thing
without being told."
-Victor Hugo

HOW TO SET YOUR COMPANY APART AND DO RIGHT BY YOUR CUSTOMERS

ELIMINATE SHORTCUTS **1**

THROW OUT
THE FINE PRINT **2**

GO ABOVE AND BEYOND **3**

PROMOTE REALNESS,
NOT PERFECTION **4**

HIRE AND TRAIN FOR
BELIEFS AND CULTURE **5**

"One factor more than any other drives whether customers recommend a builder to a friend: Feeling like the builder cares about them. For example, Rausch Coleman Homes had a customer who wrote about two frustrating problems that took a few weeks to fix after closing. But instead of giving a dissatisfied rating, they marked a near perfect 99%. The builder had made a mistake, but through an incredible response, they proved they cared. If we have intimacy and trust with the buyer, they will be happy as long as we handle mistakes well. This is true service certainty."

—Paul

To become the stuff of legend, you have to really, really set yourself apart. You can't just have a good return policy, for example; you have to have a 365-day return policy. Your internal values must be so much a part of each builder representative that the external culture reflects those beliefs. Contrary to the average homebuilder, your company must encourage the above and beyond to the point of ridiculousness—like sending customers flowers following a death in the family or spending six hours on the phone (cheerfully) with a high-maintenance caller. You have to look at your primary product as customer service and consider every hiring decision through the lens of whether or not the person is a fit for your culture. This is when you leave the world of solid customer service and find a whole new level. This is the stuff of legend—the ultimate in service certainty.

The above examples are not some pie-in-the sky idealisms. They're from the online retailer Zappos, which has made itself profitable despite offering free return shipping and defying the industry norm of limiting call length. They focus instead on building an emotional connection with each customer. This is what drives employees to have six-hour customer service calls or send flowers to a grieving customer. The customer in this case, who couldn't send her return as quickly as she'd hoped, is now as loyal as a customer gets. Zappos CEO, Tony Hsieh, says, "Looking at every one of our interactions through a branding lens instead of an expense-minimizing lens means that we run our call center very differently from others."[35]

Follow these five steps to set your company apart and do right by your customers:

1) Eliminate shortcuts.

We can find a lot of ways to pat ourselves on the back (manipulating buyers into giving positive survey scores, for example) and to create the appearance of positive customer experiences. And while such shortcuts can produce superficial results, only an inside-out approach causes employees to make the kind of out-of-the-box decisions that make the Zappos brand what it is. Zappos customers are some of the most loyal in the business. They've made the company their go-to source for shoes as well as a topic of conversation among friends and family. This kind of word-of-mouth is more valuable than any billboard or magazine ad and is therefore where Zappos invests its marketing dollars. It is their marketing.[36]

Hsieh explains, "I attribute most of our growth over the past few years to the fact that we invested time, money, and resources in three key areas: customer service, company culture, and employee training and development."[37] The investment always pays off—for both you and your customers.

2) Throw out the fine print.

Remember the company whose relationship with a homebuyer went sour over what began as a mechanical issue? If they'd handled the issue differently, they may have had a raving fan on their hands instead of a PR nightmare. Our industry lives by fine print. Many a lawyer has gotten rich writing airtight contracts to protect homebuilders from every imaginable circumstance. But even when the signed document says you don't owe a service, consider the golden rule: if it were your house, what would you want someone to do? There's a time to follow the rules (minute details obscured in dozens of pages of expectations and who's-doing-whats), and there's a time to scrap the fine print and put your customers first.

3) Go above and beyond.

In stark contrast to the penny-pinching approach many builders take, particularly with warranty requests, Denver-based Thrive Home Builders is committed to making customers happy—at all costs. Owner and CEO Gene Myers wholeheartedly believes their company mantra: "Always do the right thing."[38] These aren't just empty words or a marketing ploy. Thrive has earned repeated awards[39] and outstanding customer service scores[40] because they walk the talk.

Think beyond the gift basket.

For example, there were major warranty issues with a home they'd built for a young couple. The plumbing wasn't quite right and the roof had developed a leak. In addition to their struggles with the home, the couple had just experienced a devastating personal loss and expressed their frustration that they just couldn't seem to catch a break. Myers met with them personally and listened to their heartbreaking story. He didn't need to step away or crunch numbers to know what to do. On the spot, he told them, "You're about to catch your first break." He offered to help them sell their home and build them a new one.[41] He did it, as he says, simply because it was the right thing to do.

Going above and beyond for your customers isn't just the right thing to do—it's good business. Although Myers still doesn't know the dollar amount that new townhome cost, he says his decision has already paid off.

Thrive's most loyal Realtor heard about their unprecedented gift and offered to pitch in and help sell the original home. In the agent's words, "That's the difference between working with Thrive and any other builder. Every other builder would have just gone by the book." This example proves Myers' belief that

"Customer service is not an expense; it's an investment." This act of generosity not only made things better for Thrive's customers, but cemented their relationship with a high-volume Realtor.

4) Promote realness, not perfection.

Customers are more interested in authenticity than perfection. Have you ever wondered why reality programs are so popular, even though the quality of production is lower and the storylines are worse than in scripted programs? People watch reality shows looking for something that portrays real life. When reality shows are exposed for being staged, their ratings plummet. Everything from such TV shows to Amazon and Yelp reviews have been manipulated to the point where consumers don't know what to believe.[42] People don't mind when builders make mistakes, they just want to know you will be there for them and make it right when you do. Homebuyers are willing to accept humanity—but never dishonesty.

Don't fall into the trap of faking customer reviews or using review scrubbing services to selectively post only positive responses. Besides risking punishment by the FTC or your state DA for violation of consumer protection rights, potential customers will see you as untrustworthy. Once trust is gone, you rarely get it back. Just observe Volkswagen. They are suffering greatly for faking their diesel ratings, all in the name of beating the competition.

Authenticity is key. Align your company with a research provider that will protect your organization and the integrity of your reputation. Customers want certainty—not perfection.

5) Hire and train for beliefs and culture.

Day in and day out, Thrive Home Builders lives up to its unwavering commitment to do the right thing. In order to apply this principle in every decision, they have built a culture of believers. The employees are inspired to work for a company that truly stands out from the norm. It is a culture built around innovation, and as Myers explains, innovation is a challenge, so they need a team that is committed to the vision—committed to doing the right thing. There have even been times Myers has made the difficult decision to let go of outstanding performers who hadn't bought into the company's culture. Protecting the bigger picture is more important than pro-tecting an individual who performs well on paper, but contradicts company values or compromises the culture. He urges leaders to have courage in their convictions. It's essential for every employee to live out the culture.

At Thrive, employees are drawn to the good they do—like building houses for homeless veterans and single moms, and giving away a house to the Challenge Foundation,[43] for example. Customers and employees alike feel good about working with a business that genuinely cares.

Perhaps Myers best summarized his driving principle when he said, "People matter. I can't change the world, I can't change the industry, but I can change the lives of our homeowners. I can change the lives of our employees."[44] For him and for his small but powerful homebuilding company, it has never been just about making a buck. It has always been about creating change—one sale, one home at a time.

"The culture IS the brand," says Myers. "It's something we have to own and live out every day. We want to be open, authentic, trusted."[45]

~

Investing in customer service, company culture, and employee development pays off in spades. Your external brand is a reflection of your internal culture—so start with your culture and get your employees behind its vision. By all means, do train employees on the how-tos. Just remember that creating an experience buyers will have no choice but to rave about (and return to again and again) runs deeper and requires an all-in, total commitment to doing right by each customer. There are no shortcuts and no excuses.

When you do service right, you lower warranty costs, earn positive reviews, and keep the sale sold. Culture is the backbone of service certainty and exceptional customer service is the result. Make your primary product customer service and you'll create service certainty and the kind of customer loyalty no amount of money can buy.

[35] Tony Hsieh, "How I Did It: Zappos's CEO on Going to Extremes for Customers," *Harvard Business Review*, July-August 2010, https://hbr.org/2010/07/how-i-did-it-zapposs-ceo-on-going-to-extremes-for-customers.

[36] "How Excellent Customer Service Can Lead to More Sales," *Ecommerce Rules*, accessed August 21, 2015, http://ecommercerules.com/excellent-customer-service-can-lead-sales/.

[37] Hsieh, "How I Did It."

[38] Gene Myers, interview by Alicia Sample East, December 21, 2016.

[39] See Appendix for a sampling of awards, as provided by Stephen Myers, VP of Sales and Marketing.

[40] "Thrive Home Builders Report," Avid Ratings, accessed April 14, 2016, http://www.avidratings.com/reviews/thrive-home-builders.

[41] Gene Myers, interview by Alicia Sample East, December 21, 2016.

[42] The hit show *Keeping Up With the Kardashians* illustrates this point. See the following: Alexis Tereszcuk, " 'KUWTK' Ratings Freefall – Has Kris Jenner's Fakery Ruined The Show?," December 24, 2015, http://radaronline.com/celebrity-news/keeping-up-with-the-kardashians-ratings-freefall-kris-jenner-fake-scenes-ruining-show/.

[43] The Challenge Foundation is a non-profit that mentors students to help them break the poverty cycle. See website for further information: thechallengefoundation.org.

[44] Gene Myers, interview.

[45] Ibid.

About the Authors

Jason Forrest

With a decade of coaching and speaking experience, Jason Forrest is a member of the acclaimed National Speakers Association's Million Dollar Speakers Group (fewer than 200 people qualify) and The Entrepreneurs' Organization (EO), Fort Worth Chapter. As a leading authority in culture change programs and an expert at creating high-performance sales cultures through complete training programs, Jason starts from the top down and incorporates experiential learning to increase sales, implement cultural accountability, and transform companies into sales organizations. FPG leads homebuilders to increase profitability by creating unleavable cultures, corporate athletes, and addicted, raving fans.

As Chief Beliefs Officer at FPG, Jason's sales training philosophy comes from the belief that even the best leaders need coaching and that true, sustainable change begins at the top, occurs from the inside out, and requires long-term coaching rather than short-term training. Jason focuses on coaching organizations to increase sales and retention rates through training focused on the whole system—from CEO and president to mailroom employees.

Jason's competitive distinction is his behavior modification approach to training as applied to a variety of programs, education, and seminars, all aimed at dramatically increasing an organization's success. He's been praised by his clients—including leading homebuilders in the United States, Canada, Australia, and Mexico—for his ability to transform company cultures.

A regular contributor to national publications, Jason is also the author of *Creating Urgency in a Non-Urgent Housing Market, 40-Day Sales Dare for New Home Sales*, and *Leadership Sales Coaching*, which is the only book ever created that transforms managers into coaches. The book is listed on the Selling Power Best Books for Sales Success 2013 and was a finalist for both the Next Generation Indie Book Awards and the USA Best Book Awards.

Jason has spoken at industry events such as The International Builders' Show, PCBC, The Sunbelt Builders Show, and several of the National Association of Home Builders' (NAHB) Builder 20 Groups. He is also a member of NAHB and the Home Builders Association of Greater Dallas.

Jason was one of Training magazine's Top Ten Young Trainers of 2012. He was selected from among 1,100 entries worldwide as the winner of a 2013 Gold Stevie® Award in the Sales Training Leader of the Year category. He also won the Gold Stevie® Award for Sales Training Program of the Year and in 2015 for Sales Coaching Program of the Year.

Paul Cardis

In early 1992, Paul Cardis founded Avid Ratings, a research and consulting firm specializing in the homebuilding industry that was named a Top 50 Most Influential Technology Company by Constructech Magazine in 2014 and 2015. Since its inception, Avid Ratings has helped thousands of companies measure and improve customer loyalty, while connecting leading companies with consumers through Avid's "100% Verified Ratings." As the world's largest provider of customer research and integrated marketing for the construction industry, Avid works with more than 2,300 homebuilders and hundreds of remodelers/contractors in the United States and Canada, receiving over 1,2 million online visits from homebuyers to take surveys and learn more about its clients every year. Avid Ratings' "voice of the customer" solution (GoSurvey®) and customer engagement technology (GoTour®) enable construction companies throughout the U.S. and Canada to harness the power of authentic positive referrals to increase sales. Notably, Avid is a leading advocate of company transparency through the honest disclosure of customer reviews, and a vigilant activist to stop review fraud and review scrubbing (publishing fabricated or altered star ratings in search engines).

Paul's contributions to the industry are highly regarded by his peers. He has published over 150 articles in leading print magazines and authored cover stories on customer experience for *Professional Builder* magazine five years in a row. Paul's work has also been highlighted in the major media, including *Time* magazine, Marketwatch, MSN, Yahoo, the *Washington Post*, AZCentral, Nation's Building News, and hundreds of other websites, local newspapers, HBA newsletters, and local television broadcasts.

Paul is a regular speaker at major residential construction industry events, including The International Builders' Show, Pacific Coast Builders Conference (PCBC), South East Building Conference (SEBC), Professional Builder Benchmark Conference, Housing Leadership Summit, Big Builder, and the Avid Conference®. He also conducts regular educational sessions for his clients, NAHB Builder 20 Clubs, and private groups throughout North America.

Paul holds two master's degrees—one in educational psychology from the University of Wisconsin-Madison and one in statistics from the University of Northern Iowa.

Acknowledgments

I would like to acknowledge the entire Avid Team who over the past two-plus decades enabled me to co-write this book. If it weren't for their steadfast efforts and trust in the company, we would not have the privilege of helping so many leading builders be trusted by millions of consumers throughout North America. I also would like to thank my dearest wife and children for their support of my long hours, short weekends, and late dinners so I could squeeze in that extra effort to make this book a reality. Without the support of my loving family, none of this would be possible.

Yours Truly,

Paul Cardis

Paul Cardis

~

Thanks to the FPG team for executing the company's ideas and to the clients who have trusted us to transform your cultures.

Thank you as ever to Shelly, Saunders, and Mary Jane for your unending support.

Special thanks to Alicia Sample East for bringing these concepts to life and accepting the challenge of collaborating with two authors at the same time.

Thank you to Laura Casciano for her supervision in the creation of this entire project. Without her, this book would have never made it to print.

Jason Forrest

Jason Forrest

Appendix

Sampling of Awards for Thrive Home Builders

2016

- Grand Winner Housing Innovation, Multifamily US Dept of Energy (DOE)
- Housing Innovation Award , Multifamily, DOE
- Housing Innovation Award, Single Family, DOE
- MAME Best Green Home, Home Builders Association Metro Denver
- 2016 Builder of the Year, Green Home Builder magazine

2015

- 2015 DOE Zero Energy Ready Home Housing Innovation Award –
  U.S. Department of Energy (3rd Year in a Row)
- National Best Green Home Design 2015 – National Association of Homebuilders
- Best in Green Award 2015 – Best in Green Single Family Production Homes

2014

- 2014 Housing Innovation Award – Grand Winner –
  U.S. Department of Energy (2nd Year in a Row)
- 2014 DOE Zero Energy Ready Home Housing Innovation Award –
  U.S. Department of Energy (2nd Year in a Row)
- Green Home of the Year – MAME Award 2014 –
  HBA of Metro Denver (3rd Year in a Row)
- Energy Star® Market Leader Award 2014 –
  U.S. Environmental Protection Agency

2013

- 2013 Housing Innovation Award – Grand Winner –
  U.S. Department of Energy
- 2013 DOE Challenge Home Award –
  U.S. Department of Energy
- Green Home of the Year – MAME Award 2013 –
  HBA of Metro Denver
- Energy Star® Market Leader Award 2013 –
  U.S. Environmental Protection Agency

2012

- Green Home of the Year – Green Builder Magazine
- Green Home of the Year – MAME Award 2012 –
  HBA of Metro Denver

Bibliography

Bell, Chip. *Sprinkles.* Austin: Greenleaf Book Group Press, 2015.

Bell, Chip and Ron Zemke. *Knock Your Socks Off Service Recovery.* New York: AMACOM, 2000.

Cardis, Paul. "If You Can't Give Me All 6's." *Professional Builder.* September 1, 2005. http://www.probuilder.com/if-you-cant-give-me-all-6s.

Cardis, Paul. "Why it Pays for Homebuilders to Work with Their Toughest Customers." *Professional Builder.* July 1, 2008. http://www.probuilder.com/why-it-pays-homebuilders-work-their-toughest-customers.

Ciotti, Gregory. "How Disney Creates Magical Experiences (and a 70% Return Rate)." *Help Scout.* June 11, 2004. http://www.helpscout.net/blog/disney-customer-experience/.

Cohen, Alex. "Sprint Drops Customers Who Call for Help Too Often." *NPR.* July 11, 2007. http://www.npr.org/templates/story/story.php?storyId=11873017.

Dada, Gerardo. "Customer Centricity as Sprint's Turnaround Strategy." *Bazaarvoice.* July 6, 2010. http://blog.bazaarvoice.com/2010/07/06/customer-centricity-as-sprints-turnaround-strategy/.

Dyer, Wayne. "When you Change the Way you Look at Things." Video file. April 19, 2008. https://www.youtube.com/watch?v=urQPraeeY0w.

Federal Trade Commission. "Guides Concerning the Use of Endorsements and Testimonials in Advertising." PDF file. Last updated September 9, 2016. https://www.ftc.gov/sites/default/files/attachments/press-releases/ftc-publishes-final-guides-governing-endorsements-testimonials/091005revisedendorsementguides.pdf.

Fisher, R. J. "Social Desirability Bias and the Validity of Indirect Questioning." *Journal of Consumer Research,* 20 (1993) 303-315. https://www.mendeley.com/catalog/social-indirect-desirability-questioning-bias-validity/.

Gallup. "Five Ways to Improve Employee Engagement." *Gallup Business Journal.* January 7, 2014. http://www.gallup.com/businessjournal/166667/five-ways-improve-employee-engagement.aspx.

Gallup. "Living the brand: Beyond T-shirts: The Case for Brand Talent." *Gallup Business Journal.* November 6, 2000. http://www.gallup.com/businessjournal/208/living-brand.aspx.

Gschwandtner, L.B. "Joe Girard." *Selling Power.* Accessed June 15, 2015. http://www.sellingpower.com/content/article/?a=8598/joe-girard/&page=2.

Harmon, Katherine. "How Important is Physical Contact with your Infant?" *Scientific American.* May 6, 2010. http://www.scientificamerican.com/article/infant-touch/.

Hsieh, Tony. "How I Did It: Zappos CEO on Going to Extremes for Customers." *Harvard Business Review.* July-August 2010. https://hbr.org/2010/07/how-i-did-it-zapposs-ceo-on-going-to-extremes-for-customers.

"Man who Shot Pope John Paul II Visits his Tomb." *CBS News*. December 27, 2014. http://www.cbsnews.com/news/man-who-shot-pope-john-paul-ii-visits-his-tomb/.

Miss Cellania. "The Real Life Soup Nazi." *Neatorama*. May 15, 2014. http://www.neatorama.com/2014/05/15/The-Real-Life-Soup-Nazi/.

NASA. "Lighting Really Does Strike More Than Twice." *NASA*. January 14, 2003. http://www.nasa.gov/centers/goddard/news/topstory/2003/0107lightning.html.

Revelle, Jack. Quality Essentials: *A Reference Guide from A to Z*. ASQ Quality Press, 2004.pp. 90-93"Kano Model Tutorial." *ASQ*. Accessed February 4, 2016, http://asq.org/learn-about-quality/qfd-quality-function-deployment/overview/kano-model.html.

Rubin, Courtney. "FTC Settles First Case in New Crackdown on Fake Reviews." *Inc.* August 27, 2010. http://www.inc.com/news/articles/2010/08/ftc-settles-case-over-fraudulent-reviews.html.

"Severe Weather 101 - Lightning," *National Severe Storms Laboratory*, accessed June 19, 2016, http://www.nssl.noaa.gov/education/svrwx101/lightning/faq/.

Streitfeld, David. "Give Yourself 5 Stars? Online, it Might Cost You." *The New York Times*. September 22, 2013. http://mobile.nytimes.com/2013/09/23/technology/give-yourself-4-stars-online-it-might-cost-you.html?referrer=&_r=2.

"Thrive Home Builders Report." *Avid Ratings*. Accessed April 14, 2016. http://www.avidratings.com/reviews/thrive-home-builders.

Walker Information. "The Walker Loyalty Report for Loyalty in the Workplace." PDF file. 3. September 2007. http://www.walkerinfo.com/employeeloyalty/Employee_ExecSummary.pdf.

Ward Auto Group. "Ward Auto Dealer 500." PDF file. 2012. http://wardsauto.com/site-files/wardsauto.com/files/uploads/2012/05/UsaDe04_2012.pdf.

Wilson, Amy. "Joe Girard, a Man for the Record Books, Sold 13,001 Chevrolets in 15 Years." *Automotive News*. October 31, 2011. http://www.autonews.com/article/20111031/CHEVY100/310319926/joe-girard-a-man-for-the-record-books-sold-13001-chevrolets-in-15.

Wortham, Jenna. "For Sprint Nextel, a Drop in Customers and Earnings," *The New York Times*. February 19, 2009. http://www.nytimes.com/2009/02/20/technology/20sprint.html?_r=0.

Yi Joseph. "How Excellent Customer Service Can Lead to More Sales." *E Commerce Rules*. Accessed August 21, 2015. http://ecommercerules.com/excellent-customer-service-can- lead-sales/.

SERVICE CERTAINTY

The Service Certainty 13-week program belongs to the Service Unleashed® suite of training courses designed to equip builders, realtors, and new home sales professionals with proven techniques, behavioral strategies, and practical tools necessary to unleash their organization's peak service potential.

This program consists of an on-site full-day seminar followed by 13 weeks of participant webinars with study guides, online learning group huddles, and coaching calls.

1   Gain important skills on how to deliver the type of customer experience that ensures your buyers loyalty and advocacy. No more avoiding a chance to be extraordinary!

2   Learn that your customer service scores have more to do with your beliefs than your behaviors. You must view your customers as if they were still prospects!

3   Acquire the confidence to assertively connect with all customers, even when they are angry. No more passing the buck or avoiding conflict!

4   Understand that your goal is to create addicted, raving fans. Follow the 5 Steps to Creating Customer Intimacy and you'll have customers who not only rave about your extraordinary service – they'll actively refer their friends and family!

ABOUT FPG

Forrest Performance Group (FPG) is a global leader and designer of sales training, management training, and corporate training programs. FPG believes that true, permanent change begins at the top, transforms from the inside out, and requires long-term coaching and accountability rather than short-term training. This belief system has led to accolades for FPG, the most notable of which was their placement on the 2016 Inc. 5000 list, the most prestigious ranking of the nation's fastest-growing private companies.

Amplify

Review Builder™ automatically sings your highest praises on GoogleReviews, Yelp, Houzz, etc. and Avid Reports equips Facebook and Twitter with positive customer comments.

Avid®
Ratings

Leverage your reviews with Avid Ratings

gosocial™